LIVING AFTER A DEATH

LIVING AFTER A DEATH

A Guide for the Bereaved

Mary Paula Walsh

VERITAS

First published by The Columba Press, 1995
Published 2000 by
Veritas Publications
7/8 Lower Abbey Street
Dublin 1

ISBN 1 85390 560 7

British Library Cataloguing
in Publication Data.
A catalogue record for
this book is available
from the British Library.

The publisher and author gratefully acknowledge the
permission of Faber and Faber Ltd, and the Eliot Estate, to use
a quotation from 'East Croker' from *Collected Poems 1909-1962*
by T.S. Eliot.

Cover design by Bill Bolger
Printed in the Republic of Ireland by Betaprint Ltd, Dublin

CONTENTS

*For my parents, Doreen and Pat,
who, through their lives and deaths,
taught me so much.*

PREFACE

My father died suddenly when I was ten. He went out one Saturday afternoon with his three friends and never came back. I never said goodbye to him. A few months before that, my aunt, who lived next door, was killed in an accident, and two years before that, another aunt from next door died suddenly.

When my father died, my mother was too upset to have much attention for me. As an only child, I felt I had no one to talk to or cry with. I didn't see my father's body after he died, or go to his funeral. I never cried. I pretended I was fine. For years afterwards, I wouldn't allow anyone to talk about my father. If they did, I left the room. I was terrified I would 'break down' in front of someone. Inside I was in agony, aching and longing to cry, but not trusting anyone enough to fall apart, to show my vulnerability.

A day or two after the funeral I remember feeling particularly bad and walking out into the garden. I stood quietly. The pain was unbearable, and there seemed to be no way out. I was trapped by the pain. I struggled and fought in my head for a way out other than crying. Suddenly it seemed that there *was* an escape. I felt myself take charge of myself, of my situation – *I made a decision.* That decision was my way out. I decided that when I grew up I would do *something* so that other people would never have to feel like I was feeling then.

This book is that 'something'. Really, it is a *part* of that something, but for me a very important part. I hope it fulfils its purpose, that no one need ever feel as bad or alone as I did that day in the garden over forty years ago. At the very least they – you – will have this book for a companion. I hope it will do a great deal more.

ACKNOWLEDGEMENTS

The first person who suggested I write a book on bereavement was Ciana Campbell, a presenter on RTE's 'Twelve To One' programme on which I had been a guest. Without that invitation I would never have begun. It took over two years to complete but the journey began many, many years ago. All those who have been part of this journey have contributed – family, friends, teachers, colleagues, mentors, gurus. I could not possibly mention them all. My parents were extremely important, of course, as was the influence of my godmother, Flora Kathryn.

My introduction to Re-evaluation Counselling by Raymond Cadwell, and the founder of that organisation and author of many books, Harvey Jackins, and all the members of the International RC Community, initiated and shaped my training in counselling. My association and training with Elisabeth Kübler-Ross and Sharon Tobin were key, as was my involvement in the founding group of the Bereavement Counselling Service. Most important among them were my friends and colleagues Delma Sweeney and Tony Walsh.

A large number of friends and colleagues, too many to mention, have encouraged, helped and supported me in the actual task of researching and writing. Space allows me only to mention those without whom I would never have achieved what is such an important milestone in my own personal development. They are: Kay Conroy; Helen Crowley; Pauline Eccles; Anne Louise Gilligan; Anne Good; Gráinne Healy; Peadar Kirby; Maura Lundberg; David Louis Magee; Colette Ní Mhoitleigh; Risteárd Ó Glaisne; Mary Prenderville, Val Roche, Delma Sweeney and Katherine Zappone.

I would also like to thank all those still alive and others gone before us, mentioned either anonymously or by name in the text, whose experiences and comments were so important in bringing this book to life, particularly all my clients, past and present.

I am indebted to Jennifer Jennings and Phyllis McDonnell for their meticulous typing and to John Corcoran for tireless proofreading.

Lastly, and most importantly, thank you Kay, *anamchara*, for sharing your wisdom and strength in the face of life's mysteries, and for your persistent encouragement and support throughout this particular stage of the journey…

INTRODUCTION

GRIEVING: AN OVERVIEW

Bereavement as a Turning Point

Many of the feelings associated with loss and bereavement are most unpleasant to experience. Losing someone close to us can shake the very roots of our existence, threaten our current identity, and bring up for reappraisal our deepest beliefs and values. The death of someone in our family or immediate circle is a major life crisis, which according to the Chinese, brings both danger and opportunity.

Identity

When our existence and identity are threatened, we, as whole beings, experience threat. We experience the usual range of feelings when danger threatens – fear, followed by fight or flight. In the threatening crisis of bereavement, it is no different. We experience many feelings, but fear, anger (fight) and denial (flight) are some of the strongest.

As humans we are social animals and develop our identity in a social context, i.e. in relation to, and with, other humans. Who we are is partly determined by our relationships – attachments to others – parents, siblings, spouses, partners, children, colleagues and comrades. When we have to separate from someone, we are forced to adapt or change our identity to some extent. An obvious example of this was the widow in Victorian times, whose social identity was dependent solely on her husband. When he died she became a social outcast. In some cultures this was so strong that the widow was obliged to die also – she had no separate role in society. Happily that is changing, at different paces in different cultures. I often think of the lines from the old song, 'Every time I say goodbye, I die a little'. It is in fact part of us that dies – part of our identity, which is part of who we are – part of existence as we experience it. Naturally, therefore, we feel threatened.

Beliefs

No matter how strong our religious faith, no matter how spiritually developed we are, the meaning of death remains a mystery, as does the meaning of life; both, of course, being inextricably linked.

We humans seem to need meaning in order to live. 'He who has a "why" to live, can bear with almost any "how"'. A brush with bereavement or death can shake the very foundations of 'why'. After all, even a long life can appear as just the twinkling of an eye, especially in the case of a tragic or accidental death, or that of a foetus, baby or young person.

Values

Closely tied to meaning are values, which help us to organise our lives and prioritise. They influence our choices of lifestyle, friends, partners and work or careers. Faced with the many feelings death can evoke, such as helplessness and loss of control, values previously held can disappear overnight, or appear trite and meaningless.

Opportunity

In order to grow as a whole person, to reach our full potential or as near as possible, we must change. Growth is a process of continual change. As the plant needs the stimulus of water and sun to grow, we humans need stimuli. Life presents us with many stimuli; some, such as hormonal changes, come from within, and many and various life events, such as birth, schoolwork, social situations and relationships, come from outside ourselves.

Most of these changes occur without looking for them. Many occur 'naturally'. Some changes we take on voluntarily in order to achieve or gain something, or even simply 'for the hell of it', for fun or adventure. Bereavement also causes changes in our lives, not only in identity, beliefs and values, but in many practical ways, such as how, where or with whom we live.

It is possible to live through many of these types of changes without growing, i.e. without changing ourselves, or by changing only barely enough to survive.

Growth

What often happens is that, for reasons dealt with elsewhere in this book, we fail to let go of old identities, beliefs, values, relationships or lifestyles. We fail to change in a changing world; we fail to move on, to grow. This may result from a combination of attitude or perspective, with a lack of ability to change, due to unfinished business from the past. This unfinished business may be either ungrieved losses or separations, or bad experiences with past attachments.

Turning point

Bereavement can be regarded as a turning point or opportunity for growth. The advantages of this choice of perspective are as follows:

- We learn more about our identity – who we are. I do not wish to imply that the crisis of bereavement is a positive experience in itself, but that we are free to choose to regard it as an opportunity for growth, and an opening to the adventure that is life.
- We question our beliefs and values so that we can discard those we regard as outdated or those no longer useful, and strengthen those we have found to be truly important.
- We can, because of the above two advantages, see life differently, i.e. 'put on a new pair of spectacles'. Surely, the more different pairs we have, or ways we can look at the world, the more flexible and, therefore, open, we can be, the more exciting life is, and the more possibilities we can see. We are therefore able to enjoy life more, see more opportunities, and have more adventures.
- We can make new and perhaps better relationships with people, places and things.
- We can be prepared to cope better with future losses.

Attachment and Separation – a Continuum

There are so many ways of looking at the mysterious journey of life, which we are all travelling. Since becoming involved in bereavement work, I have found that one useful way to look at it is as a series of attachments and separations or losses.

We begin life as the attachment or coming together of a sperm and an ovum, as a little organism that attaches itself to the wall of the womb, only to separate again after nine months, when we as an entity make our first major separation, the physical separation from our mother at our birth.

We then have to learn to live a separate existence from her, and the separation progresses in stages, from weaning, through crèche or playgroup, pre-school, primary and secondary school, to leaving home in late teens or early twenties, and usually subsequent emotional separation.

Meanwhile, on the journey, we have attached to many other humans, such as our father, siblings, grandparents, carers, teachers and friends, lovers, spouses and partners. Of course we also make many other attachments besides people – possessions of all sorts, houses, pets, places, countries, ideas, ideals, dreams and ambitions.

Effects of Past Attachments and Separations

Though our grieving varies enormously, depending on how attached we were to whatever has been lost, many of the feelings that loss and separation evoke are similar, whether it was to a person or any of those things.

For the purpose of this book on bereavement, I will focus on loss of a person through death. The way in which we have grieved for other things, as well as persons, in the past, may affect how we grieve for persons in the present or future.

Whether we make successful attachments, and manage to grieve and let go of people who have died, depends, to a large extent, on our early experience of these processes.

Positive experiences of attachment

If our early experience of attachment – most importantly, to our biological mother, but also to a main carer and significant others, such as father, grandparents and siblings – has been positive, we may dare to attach again and again as we journey through life. Most of us cannot 'remember' whether our early attachments were positive in the way we can 'remember' what we did last week. But a 'sense' of these early experiences remains in our subconscious to influence our adult behaviour.

Negative experiences of attachment

If the experience was negative, decisions about attachment will stir up negative connotations, and we will 'think twice' about attaching again – maybe even about making decisions in general. If this happens, we may try to hold on to what has been lost, even if the relationship was not a good one, rather than risk the pain of a new attachment: 'the devil you know is better than the devil you don't!'

You may have difficulty in making new relationships if you sense that your early experience of relationship was any or all of the following. If the early experience:

- lacked physical closeness – the nurturing of being held and cuddled;
- was abusive – physically, sexually, spiritually or emotionally;
- failed to allow you to feel loved, without having to give something back;
- was of being abandoned, either through death or other separation.

If any of these were your experience, and you feel that it is inhibiting you in your relationships, talk it over with a friend or perhaps a counsellor or a psychotherapist.

Loss/separation

As negative experience of early attachments affects adult relationships, so it is with loss/separation. If you were unable to grieve losses/separations in your past for any reason, it may affect your ability to grieve in adult life.

If you have difficulty in facing the reality of your loss, in grieving, in adjusting to life without the deceased, or in stepping out into a new life and/or relationship, maybe you have experienced some of the following early losses/separations:

- You never or seldom cried when separating, or after the loss of anyone or anything.

- Your family pretended nothing had happened when someone, or even a pet, died.
- Your family negated the loss by pretending everything was 'fine' when someone died, and rationalised it, e.g. 'she was old/in pain/going to heaven/our of her misery', etc.

Again, if you have a sense of having experienced one or all of the above in early childhood, and you feel you are becoming 'stuck' with an old bereavement, talk it over with a friend, counsellor or psychotherapist.

Grieving: A Natural Process

Grieving is a natural process. It is an in-built human healing mechanism which, when not damaged or inhibited, allows us to face our loss; feel whatever feelings it has evoked; let go; adjust to life without what has been lost, and re-attach to new persons or things.

In-built healing mechanism

Have you ever noticed a small child when she falls and hurts herself? The first thing she does is pick herself up, if able, and then she finds a familiar loving adult, runs to her and begins to cry. If the child cannot immediately find a person, she will 'hold' the tears till she does, even until she gets home to her mother or carer. The child will then proceed (no one has to tell her what to do) to cry for quite a long time, maybe even shaking at the same time, then maybe rage, and eventually, if uninterrupted, talk about what happened, sometimes in detail, repeating herself over and over again. If still uninterrupted, she will eventually slow down and stop the grieving process, look for a hug or cuddle, and then run off and play as if nothing had ever happened.

If this process is allowed to happen, and the child is allowed, and, if necessary, encouraged, to complete it, she will carry no harmful effects from the hurtful experience, in this case, the fall.

Sadly, however, because our parents were rarely allowed to grieve in such a way, they could not listen to the grieving that was necessary to complete the healing for us as children. Their own 'inner children' are still bottling up inexpressed grief, which is brought to the surface by listening to others grieving.

They found all kinds of ways to stop or inhibit us, either angrily ('Stop that or I will give you something to cry about!'), or 'kindly', by distracting our attention, giving us sweets, hugging us tightly or showing us something exciting to play with. They rewarded those who did not 'make a fuss', and punished those who did.

Early influences

You can understand by now that most of us have had this in-built healing mechanism damaged to some degree, varying according to our gender, culture, religious customs, individual upbringing and life history. These early experiences are powerful teachers, and we are influenced by them in a way we never are at a later stage. This may be because they are closely tied up with our survival. The most important thing for tiny children is to see that they are kept alive, and they are totally dependent on adults for this, i.e. keeping the adults attentive to the needs vital for survival. No wonder we are quick to learn pleasing behaviour!

This situation is not irreversible. Reviving this healing mechanism we all possess is just that: *re-viving*. We still have the ability – it has just become rusty and unexercised!

Men and women

Men and women seem to grieve differently in some ways. We cannot be sure how much of this is due to genetic or biological difference, and how much is due to conditioning. In the case of grieving, which involves so much expression of feelings, much of the difference between men and women appears to be conditioned, i.e. it has been learned in various ways.

In our society men are taught to hide their feelings, to be 'tough' and 'brave' and 'strong'. These qualities, for some reason, are associated with lack of feeling and the 'stiff upper lip', 'brave face on it' reaction. I believe this may be due to the conditioning of hundreds of years, when men fought to protect the tribe in order to ensure its survival. Of course it is not 'soft' or 'cowardly' or 'weak' to show and express feelings, but that is how our society sometimes sees it.

Men are taught from early years to be rational and activity-orientated. Women are taught to be involved with and aware of relationships and the feeling element of human make-up and interaction. Women are given permission to express their feelings more frequently and more openly.

This view of society, of course, includes a lot of generalisation, and though it applies in many cases, there are exceptions. Also the expression of *some* feelings is acceptable from men, and *not* from women, e.g. anger.

The reasons for this kind of conditioning are complex, as is the whole question of women's oppression in our society, and its perpetuation through sexism and internalised women's oppression. It is sufficient in this context to note the differences in the grieving process, and how women and men can be helped to grieve in ways suited to them.

Culture

Each culture has its own rituals connected with death. Since most societies up until this century were largely rural, rituals were community based and provided strong support to the bereaved. Death was not denied or hidden away. The attitudes to it emphasised its inevitability and its part in the natural order of things.

In Ireland, for example, death was regarded as an important community social occasion. Social gatherings were very much part of the community ritual. The body of the deceased was usually 'laid out' at home before removal to the church, and a party was often held at the deceased person's house. This was called a 'wake'.

The advantages of the wake were many. Some were as follows:

- Children became familiar at an early age with death and dead bodies. Children used to run naturally in and out of the room where the deceased was laid out, often even playing there and giggling, which was the best way for them to get over the embarrassment and fears associated with death.
- The wake engendered a feeling of support for the deceased's family, from friends and neighbours. It was common for them to help with laying out the corpse, cleaning and tidying the house, and bringing

food, e.g. whole hams, chickens, puddings, bread, bracks, cakes – and drink. This allowed the family freedom to stay with the grieving process.

- The wake gave the family permission to grieve openly and in the company of friends and neighbours. This was a tremendous contradiction of the isolation and loneliness so frequently felt at this early stage of loss.
- The corpse or body played a central part in the 'celebration'. This allowed the family and friends to face the reality of the death early on. It continued over a period of days, rather than a quick visit to a funeral parlour or morgue, with little more than a 'peep' at the deceased.

The only disadvantage, it seems, was the abuse of alcohol, which often still occurs at the time of a death, whether or not there is a formal or traditional wake. It is used to excess to 'drown', or cut off, the unpleasant feelings death can evoke.

People today are now in a relatively new and quite different situation. Populations are largely concentrated in cities and towns. The extended family has been left behind with the rural lifestyle, and children are no longer in touch with animals, farming and the natural ways of life. They are no longer used to living with elderly relatives and watching them age and die.

Besides urbanisation, the advent of television has resulted in wide exposure to different cultural influences. Death is becoming more of a taboo than it ever was. Many more people are dying in hospitals or nursing homes. The 'American Way of Death', with funeral parlour and all its trappings, seems to be the norm. Rituals and customs surrounding death have broken down, with resulting isolation and difficulties in grieving and coping with loss.

All of this has, in the short term, increased the need for support groups, voluntary and professional grief counsellors and grief therapists. In the long term, I believe, there is a need for old customs and rituals to be revived, 'updated', and new ones created, to help people cope with this crisis.

Religious customs

In my experience, a person's religious beliefs, or absence of them, do not affect whether or not they express their grief. But religious beliefs regarding life after death are often used to rationalise a person's inability to grieve, for whatever reason.

However, religious beliefs regarding the afterlife do affect the time-span of the grieving and, most of all, the person's attitude while grieving, and the ability to recover and re-engage in life again. This may vary according to the religion, and my experience is mainly in the Christian tradition.

It depends, of course, on what you believe about suffering and death. Are they meaningless, cruel accidents, or are they of some value and/or part of an overall plan? Is death the 'final stage of growth' and so an entry into a fuller life, or is it the end, the 'final curtain'?

Some religions put a lot of emphasis on this life, some on the 'larger' life-after-death, and some on reincarnation. Some discourage the idea of individual survival in any shape or form.

In the early Christian tradition, belief in hell and punishment may have caused people to fear their own death and life thereafter. I have not found this to be an issue for the bereaved. Strangely, though we can often see hell and/or punishment of some kind as a possibility for ourselves, we rarely, if ever, contemplate anyone else, particularly our loved ones, being subjected to it.

This may be because we instinctively think well of the deceased, because we 'never speak ill of the dead', or because we tend to idealise people once they have 'crossed the divide'. In my experience, whether from a religious training and belief system or from a sense of our own and others' essential spiritual nature, some belief in either a transcendent or immanent God, or some sense of spirituality, is a source of great comfort and strength to those who are grieving.

Individual upbringing

We are, of course, raised in a social context, in which cultural and religious beliefs and customs play an important part; however, there are many differences within families about how death, dying and grieving are regarded. These range from almost total denial, to those families who can use the death of one member as an opportunity for those remaining to grow closer together.

Life history

How we have grieved each loss in the past, and whether we perceived our way of grieving as having been helpful or not, will affect how we grieve subsequently. Grieving takes courage. If we have grieved well in the past, we will grieve more boldly and more positively in the future. If we have been able to grieve, let go and move on once, we can do it again.

'Ungrieved' or unresolved losses snowball as we go through life. If early losses have left a residue of unexpressed grief, this will get re-stimulated, or we will be reminded of it again when a new loss happens. If that one, and others up to then, is not dealt with, there will be more 'snow' gathered, to be 'melted' or expressed next time.

Stages of Grief

Humans, as whole persons, have amazing ways of surviving not only physically but also mentally, emotionally and spiritually. We start with a very strong basic instinct for survival, and we develop techniques or mechanisms as we grow to defend or protect ourselves in all kinds of ways. Those we develop to protect ourselves psychologically are commonly known as 'defence mechanisms'.

When we hear 'bad news', or anything that we perceive as being threatening to the 'self', we react by going into a seemingly automatic process of self-defence. This process takes the form of allowing the news to 'dawn' on us slowly, or in stages. We 'let it in' bit by bit, all the while adjusting so that when it fully dawns, we are able to 'take' it. This protective process works somewhat differently with different people, but basically it follows a fairly typical pattern. Many writers on loss and separation have written about this process of letting in, calling it 'the stages of grief'. The expression was originally coined by Freud and, more recently, Elisabeth Kübler-Ross, who identified five stages in the following order: denial; anger; bargaining; depression; acceptance.

It is not difficult to see how these emotions are 'buffers', helping to keep the bad news at a distance at first, as you proceed to let it in slowly.

The timespan over which the whole process spreads can vary from minutes, in the case of loss of your wallet, for example, to years in the case of loss of a beloved person.

The emotions singled out by Elisabeth Kübler-Ross for the stages of grief are not the only ones we experience when grieving. In her book, *On Death and Dying*, she also identifies: isolation; guilt; fear; hope. I would add: anxiety; loneliness; abandonment; shock; fatigue; disbelief; helplessness; powerlessness; despair.

When grieving any loss, we can experience any or all of these emotions. They often seem to hit us with alarming force, and to have frightening power over how we feel and behave. They spread across the whole gamut of human emotions. I have rarely met a grieving person who has not at some stage in the process felt suicidal. Frequently I have met someone who feels intensely and vitally alive.

If the loss is something small, or unimportant to us, we still experience a whole range of feelings, but they can pass so quickly that we barely recognise that we are experiencing them, or even remember them afterwards.

Have you ever had the experience of missing an early-morning bus? The first feeling we experience is shock, then denial – we keep checking our watches, even asking people in the bus queue if it has really gone. Next we often feel anger – with the bus company usually, or with a family member for delaying us; or guilt, blaming ourselves for not getting up on time. We may then bargain with God or some vague omnipotent personage. 'Please let the bus come and I'll reform my life – get up earlier, eat less breakfast', etc. As the fact that the bus has actually gone begins to dawn on us, we begin to feel sad and realise how it will affect our day... annoy the boss. We feel helpless in that we are unable to make the bus come. Acceptance brings some sense of an end to the grieving and getting back to reality – shall I thumb a lift, get a taxi, walk, or go back to bed? Sound familiar?

Grieving is, therefore, something we do most days, sometimes several times a day, and we, probably unconsciously, take the process for granted. It is a normal reaction to experience these feelings. As the timespan of the whole process varies, so does the intensity, depending on the degree of the attachment to what has been lost.

Tasks of Mourning

A well-known author on grief, William Worden, in his book *Grief Counselling and Grief Therapy*, suggests that you can divide grief work into four tasks.

1. To accept the reality of the loss.
2. To experience the pain of grief.
3. To adjust to an environment in which the deceased is missing.
4. To withdraw emotional energy and reinvest it in another relationship.

All these tasks need to be carried out before grief work has been completed. It takes each individual a different amount of time to do this.

If you compare these 'tasks' of Worden to Elisabeth Kübler-Ross's 'stages' of grief, you can see how they match, i.e. working to accept the reality of loss equates to the first stage of denial and disbelief; experiencing the pain and adjusting to an environment in which the deceased is missing equates to anger, bargaining and depression; while withdrawing emotional energy and reinvesting it in another, would indicate acceptance.

The idea of having tasks to complete while grieving is useful. It can be helpful in counteracting feelings of powerlessness. It can also help you to break down what may seem like an interminable amount of work, into a finite number of steps, which can be 'ticked off' as you progress. However, like the 'stages', these tasks do not follow neatly in the order presented, but can be used as a guideline.

As you grieve, you will find your *own* way. This book is intended as a map. Each of you must travel your own individual journey.

PART I

FACING THE LOSS

CHAPTER 1

BAD NEWS

Breaking the News

There is no 'nice' way to hear bad news, no pleasant way to 'break' it. Most people do their best to break it gently, and all we remember afterwards is that sudden, cold feeling that seems to grip us somewhere below our heart, frequently followed by a sensation as if the bottom part of our stomach is falling out.

If the news is totally unexpected and the affected person very important to us, it can feel as if our whole world is being shaken under our feet. Our stability is being radically threatened.

If you have the difficult job of breaking 'bad news', try not to do it over the telephone. Joan, on an idyllic holiday in Greece, was called to the phone to hear, on a very bad connection, her sister saying, 'John (their brother aged thirty) is dead. You had better come home!' It might have been better to say he had an accident and was seriously injured, followed by 'I am afraid he died'. In some situations it might be better to allow the possibility that John could die to sink in on Joan's journey home, thus slightly cushioning the shock.

If you are nervous of breaking 'bad news', bring someone with you, preferably someone close or familiar to the bereaved person, to allow her to feel safe. It is bad enough to receive such a shock without having to worry about 'putting on a brave face' or being polite. It is common for someone breaking bad news to say very little and just 'hint'. In that way, the person ends up breaking it to themselves! For example, Michael calls to tell Mary that her husband John has died suddenly. 'Hello, Mary. I am afraid I have some bad news. Oh yes, I will come in.' Then he says nothing for so long and he looks so devastated that Mary begins to guess. 'Is it one of the children?' 'No.' 'Is it John?' No answer. Mary again asks if he is hurt. No answer. 'He's dead?' At last Michael says, 'I'm sorry, Mary', which is meant to mean 'Yes'. In this exchange, Mary has had to break the news to herself really.

It might have been better as follows: Michael calls, having collected Mary's best friend, Anna, and brought her along. 'Hello, Mary. Can we come in? Thanks' (comes in and sits down.) 'I am afraid I have some bad news for you. It's John. There has been an accident at work' (short pause). 'I am afraid it was very serious (short pause) and John died. He was killed instantly and didn't suffer at all.'

If someone has to go to identify a body, it is important that they go, if possible, with someone who is not too scared, or is used to dead bodies. It is never easy, but this is not a time for the relative to have to worry about her companion. The companion can be there to think about her.

Breaking news of a serious or 'terminal' illness is a different matter. This is an unpleasant job often left to 'professionals'. Remember it is no easier for them just because they are professionals and have done it many times before. They are humans with emotions, somebody's wife, husband, mother, daughter or son.

Nowadays consultants and GPs are becoming much more aware of the importance of communication. This, of course, includes communication of 'bad news'. There is a lot of discussion regarding training in communication skills at the moment and this has resulted in some improvement of the situation. Healthcare professionals in general, and doctors in particular, are much more likely to tell patients if their prognosis is bad, and that is progress. Many have not yet learned enough communication/counselling skills to do it sensitively and well. Some of the reason for this is the kind of time-constraints doctors put on themselves. It is likely, therefore, that if someone has been given bad news or a bad prognosis by a doctor, the doctor may not have taken enough time to listen to how the patient feels about that news, or to allow them to ask all the questions they wanted to ask. This can make an unpleasant, frightening experience even worse. One thing you can do: if you are going to hear the results of a test, etc., just as with breaking news of death or identification of a body, remember you do not have to face this alone.

A friend of mine had to go to get results of tests on a lump in her leg. I went with her. Beforehand we wrote a list of questions she wanted to ask. When we arrived at the surgery, she went in first and asked the consultant if her friend (me) could come in, as she was so nervous she might not hear all he had to say, or remember all the questions she wanted to ask. He agreed and they fetched me. I went in and sat quietly. I said nothing. My friend listened to what the consultant had to say and I wrote it down. Then she asked some questions from our list and I ticked them off and wrote the answers. She forgot one or two and I reminded her. The consultant shook both our hands on leaving and seemed quite happy about the whole thing – unusual though it may have been for him. Outside we went for a cup of tea and I listened to her fears and anxieties and we discussed what she should do next. She found my being there a great help, and still recalls the occasion.

If the ill person is in a hospital bed, and hears that her illness is serious or 'terminal', she can ask for the curtains to be pulled around the bed, if she wishes. Privacy can be important at this time, especially when those close next come to visit.

The first feeling we become aware of after hearing 'bad news', either of death or 'terminal' illness, is *shock*. This kind of shock produces many of the symptoms of physical shock – nausea, diarrhoea, shivering, cold or hot sweating, light headedness or dizziness and, occasionally, fainting or loss of consciousness for a very brief moment. These are perfectly natural. They are a 'normal' reaction to 'abnormal' (i.e. threatening) news. The sufferer should be treated as with any shock, with the usual first aid, i.e. gentleness, asked to sit or lie down, given a hot, sweet drink – but not alcohol or drugs – and, if faint, have the head put lower than the rest of the body, and be wrapped warmly. If you are with someone in this situation, try not to panic yourself. It helps them if you look calm and appear to be coping. Having 'come to' after the initial shock, the ill or bereaved will begin to embark on the long and painful journey ahead.

Not everyone dies from so-called 'terminal' illness. Being told you have one, or given a gloomy prognosis, is *not* a death sentence. Many people are cured, go into remission or just spontaneously recover for no apparent reason. Very occasionally, 'miracles' occur. 'Hope springs eternal' and should *never* be taken away.

As this book is about bereavement, and for the bereaved, I will approach the journeys of terminal illness and of bereavement from the viewpoint of the bereaved or 'soon-to-be-bereaved'.

The Journey of Terminal Illness

When we discover a friend or loved one has a 'terminal' illness, it brings all our own feelings about being ill and dying to the surface. The feelings are influenced by the way we were brought up, the general views of society and our own personal past experiences.

Very often, we feel embarrassed and want to avoid the ill person, or, if not, we want to avoid the subject when with them. Sometimes, it is almost as if this person we knew and loved suddenly becomes a stranger or is changed in some fundamental way. Of course they are different after such news, but no more different than after, for example, getting married or emigrating. Because we treat them as different, they feel even more isolated on this lonely journey.

Of course no one can travel it *for* them, and it may be a journey inwards – an end 'from which no traveller has returned'. But we *can* travel it *with* them, accompany them at least until they are no longer with us physically. If we decide to be a companion to such a traveller, there are many ways in which we can help shorten the road. It won't be easy. It will, though, be rewarding. I believe it to be a privilege to be accepted or trusted, to be what might be called an *anamchara* or soul-friend of this kind. Most dying people choose one person to be their special *anamchara*. Some people go to counsellors or psychotherapists, and sometimes the counsellor or therapist is chosen to be the special one, but not always. Some dying people choose their spouse or close relative, but not always. There may be too many emotional ties, making it just too painful.

If you are to be such a friend, the first and most important 'rule' is to be yourself, be natural. For most of us, it is such an effort to behave differently that the energy goes into the effort, and not into being there for the ill person. As so many people 'run' emotionally or physically in the face of terminal illness and death; just being there is the best gift you can give.

To tell or not to tell

If your friend or relative is in hospital or has had tests, sometimes you will be told the 'bad news' or prognosis before she is. You may then, for any number of reasons, be the person who has to break the news to her, if she is to be told. There is a lot of discussion currently around whether 'to tell or not to tell'. As I have said, increasingly doctors and consultants are taking on that responsibility. However, it may fall to you to tell her, or to decide whether she is to be told or not.

Each case or situation is very different. It is important to remember that, when we are fearful, we try to *control* situations, in order to control the amount of fear, or to suppress it altogether. Very often, we are not aware we are doing this, as 'flight' from fear is so natural in any threatening situation. For example, if your mother has had a lung biopsy, and the consultant tells you she has secondary lung cancer, the first thing you *might* say is, 'She mustn't be told. She couldn't cope.'

However, just for a moment, let your imagination flow and imagine the following scenario. You are a forty-five-year-old woman who has been putting on a bit of weight lately and not feeling quite 'yourself'. You think it might be menopause. You have been feeling particularly seedy in the early mornings, sometimes vomiting. You have mysteriously turned against some foods and developed an addiction for others. You go to your GP and have a few tests in hospital as an outpatient. The doctor calls in your husband to tell him the results – (she never tells *you*) that you are pregnant! You continue to put on weight, especially in certain places, and the other 'symptoms' continue. You wonder if you are pregnant, and as time goes on, become more and more sure that you must be. When asked, your husband says, 'Oh no! There is *nothing* the matter. You are fine. You will be back to your old self any day now.' No one else will discuss it, and if *you* bring it up they look upset or awkward or change the subject. As the pregnancy advances you will feel confused and will even begin to think you're imagining it. It's 'all in your head', and maybe you're going mad!

That is perhaps an exaggerated analogy, but I find it a very useful one. It highlights the feelings and predicament of the ill person. It also highlights the *relationship* with her husband, doctor and others, who *could* be her main support. The relationships have become distant – any *real* communication is avoided in case the dreaded subject comes up or questions are asked.

Most people who are seriously ill know it, at some level, though not all know at a conscious level. Often they speak in what Elisabeth

Kübler-Ross calls 'symbolic language'. If possible, we should answer in the same symbolism or metaphor. A useful metaphor we can use is that of a journey, either that of illness or of life itself.

I remember visiting a dying friend, Jo, with a colleague of mine. Jo was extremely ill and weak. Neither of us had seen her since she became ill, and M. said something like, 'It's a hard journey you're on Jo. I'm so sorry.' Jo answered that it was hard and frightening. M. responded about the fear, and so on. Neither mentioned death but both used the metaphor of the journey to talk about what, for Jo, was the indescribable. I was amazed at how deep the conversation went and how helpful it was to Jo.

Even better if the dying person is the one to choose the metaphor or symbolism and initiate the conversation. Elderly people often talk about 'going home'. We must keep very aware to notice if indeed, at some level, they are talking about a home in another dimension. Dying people often have a sense of journeying towards home. That is both mysterious and comforting for them, and also for those around them.

Never lie to a dying person, but never be *too* sure if and when they may die. We cannot be sure – ever.

They will often ask, and though I think it is important to find out how much they suspect or know, it is cruel, I believe, to play games with them. It is common for someone to ask, 'Do you think I am dying?' and for the carer or relative to answer, 'What do *you* think? Do *you* think you are?'

That's fine if they answer 'Yes' or 'No', but if they say, 'I don't know. What do you think?' What then? I would suggest saying, 'You know you are very ill, don't you? But I couldn't say definitely when you or anyone else will end the journey.' Then try to continue with a dialogue and, above all, be honest, though that does *not* mean saying *everything* you think, or know.

Listening

Try to listen and not to interrupt. This can be more difficult than it sounds, as you will soon discover. Either of two things will often happen when your friend is talking about her illness or impending death:

1. You will be reminded of similar events in your own, or your family's experience, and you will feel a strange compulsion to interrupt, or jump in with your story.

2. Or, you will feel so very embarrassed, uncomfortable, frightened or sad that you'll try to stop them in all kinds of ways. Sometimes you'll skilfully and subtly change the subject, and sometimes you will find yourself crying or saying something like, 'Oh don't say that', 'Don't talk like that', 'Don't talk about it', or even 'Of course you are going to get better. Be positive'. You may even cry so much, or have such a sad or fearful expression on your face, that it will stop them sharing with you.

We do this 'fending off' because we are denying that our friend or loved one is so ill or dying, and because it is too painful to admit to ourselves. Once we realise this, and acknowledge it to ourselves, we immediately become better listeners. In some instances, depending on your relationship with the dying person, you can tell them (*briefly*) how difficult it is for you. Crying together with someone you love about their approaching death can be a truly healing experience.

Listening to another's story brings to the surface feelings connected with similar stories of our own. This can happen in a very strong way with the subject of death and dying. That is because most of us are afraid of dying – and that's quite usual. It is quite 'normal' to be afraid of dying, and I strongly believe that the fear is far worse than the actual dying!

We can be much more helpful to a dying person if we can face and accept our own mortality, even if we are afraid.

If you are able to listen *well* to your dying friend, *without* interrupting, changing the subject, or stopping them altogether, you will be giving them an immense gift.

What can you do if you are finding it difficult? Once again, remember you are not alone. Become more aware of what is happening to *you* when you are listening to the ill or dying person. Make mental notes of what triggers you to interrupt, or to come in with your own story, or to try to stop them talking. Is it when she talks about the actual moment of dying, or her fear of pain? Is it her grief at leaving her children and family? Is it the fear she expresses in relation to her religious beliefs, to her views on the afterlife, or is it her discomfort and loss of dignity as her illness progresses?

Nearly everyone finds that feelings of fear about their own death surface from time to time. When you know what is triggering your own experience – 'pressing your buttons' – that is more than half the battle. You are not only finding out what stops you being a good listener for her, but also where your own grief and fear lie. This is a marvellous gift for your own personal growth while helping another.

So, when you have identified these unresolved experiences in your past, you can do one or all of the following:

- Find a friend to whom you can talk about those experiences.
- Write about them in your journal.
- Pray or meditate about them.
- Find a counsellor, self-help group or psychotherapist to talk to.

If you take the time and trouble to do any or all of these, you are taking good care, not only of your friend, but of yourself also.

The ill person, after the initial shock, will, in order to protect herself from too much pain, let the 'bad news' in slowly, usually starting by denial. This can take various forms, from denial of illness, or the particular illness, to denial that it is 'terminal'. Often people slip into denial and out again very fast, which can be a little disconcerting at first. It is common for someone to talk openly about fast-approaching death, from being quite clear it would be soon to, the next minute, discussing what they would be doing for Christmas!

This is because humankind 'can only bear so much reality'. Wouldn't it be very difficult to stay with the idea of impending death sixty minutes an hour, twenty-four hours a day?

If the ill person is listened to long enough, and well enough, she will gradually move through the other stages – anger, bargaining, depression – and experience probably fear, hope, guilt, powerlessness and many other feelings at different times.

If your friend, when in denial, sees other doctors apart from her original GP or consultant, or looks for second opinions, it can be very difficult to watch or to agree with. However, she will usually go back to the original doctor eventually. Second opinions can be a great ally in helping people in denial to move through it. Just try to listen patiently. It is not helpful to insist on the stark reality.

In fact, besides never knowing *for certain* if an illness is going to lead to death, neither can we, nor any doctor, know for certain when death will come. This I believe is merciful. We could all benefit from living more in the present, but this is a skill 'terminally' ill people need to develop fast. In their situation, strangely, they often do learn it faster and more easily than 'healthy' people, maybe because they perceive they have more to gain.

Because 'hope springs eternal' naturally in humans, it must never be dashed. Always encourage your dying friend or loved one to be hopeful. You may notice that as their illness progresses they will begin to hope for different things. At first it may be hope for a cure or a miracle, then a remission, then even a short period of good health, then escape from more treatment or surgery and freedom from pain. They may move on to hope for a pain-free, easy or happy death, to hope for seeing loved ones in the next life, to hope for the future of family, children or grandchildren who are left, or for particular funeral plans.

You can help them to live in the present, not by denying the future or pretending, but by making the present as comfortable, happy, interesting, or even exciting as possible, with lots of treats, all of course depending on how well they are and what they particularly enjoy. Guard against deciding for them. After all, none of us knows when we are going to die, and most of us manage to enjoy many things sometimes, even though death is certain for us all.

Positivity

I believe there is a lot of non-sense talked about 'positivity'. Often it is used as an excuse to avoid reality, sometimes to describe the stage of denial when we cannot yet bear to look at the 'negative' possibilities.

There are always two or more ways of looking at a situation. The glass is either half full or half empty. To me, positivity is the ability to see that, while it may *feel* that it is half empty, it is *in fact* half full. That attitude is not easy to keep alive and needs nurturing in ourselves. We need others around us who are of like mind.

So if your loved one has a life-threatening illness, it can be helpful in keeping hope alive to have the ability to stay positive, without denying what is actually happening.

Pretence or falseness is actually disturbing to the ill person because they will detect it immediately and feel even more isolated and abandoned in their predicament, if no one is prepared to 'journey with them'.

It is helpful for both you and them to have times when it is agreed that it is OK to be 'negative', hopeless and despairing. This will probably happen naturally at times, but do not let it go on for more than, say, an hour at a time, once or twice a day.

The immune system responds well to the outward expression of emotions. That does not mean the ill person will be cured if they express negative emotions all the time. It is exhausting. A balance is most important. The immune system also responds well to happiness, to doing what we most enjoy.

Boosting the immune system is good for general quality of life and a feeling of well-being, as well as helping to fight infection, side-effects of treatment, weakness and so on. It does not necessarily mean it is curing the core illness.

We often hear the word 'fighting' in connection with serious illness, and cancer in particular. Militaristic language was associated with the strict medical model of disease at a time when illness was seen as a state of siege, in which the healthy 'host' organism was attacked by an outside invading 'army' of germs. I am inclined now to look at it more as a state of dis-ease, brought about by the whole organism itself, for one or a number of reasons – physical, environmental, emotional, mental or spiritual. In this case, 'fighting' becomes an irrelevant concept. Recovery, or turning the situation round to one of ease or health, is an act of the whole organism in a new direction, rather than a destruction of a part. Often the organism will 'choose' or decide to take the direction of dying – exiting from this life.

After all, as things exist at present, we all must exit at some time. We might say, 'But why now?' On the other hand, 'Why not now?'

The Journey of Bereavement

No matter how long you have been expecting or waiting for someone to die, even if they have been unconscious for a long period, that sharp irreversible moment of *no going back* that is death, comes as a shock. No matter how much 'anticipatory grieving' we have done, and that does help, once we know that the moment-of-no-return has been passed, not only has the deceased changed utterly but so has the bereaved person. Her reaction is, as I have said, entirely dependent on her background, past history, and relationship to the deceased.

So *everyone* who is told news of a death will react differently. However, there are some feelings that people usually experience such as shock, numbness, isolation, loneliness, denial, bargaining, anger, guilt, fear, helplessness, sorrow, depression and despair. These will be dealt with in detail in Chapter 6.

One individual will probably not experience *all* of these feelings but it is possible they may do, even momentarily. Most of the feelings will flash through them in the first hours or after the initial numbness and denial. After that, each person will experience one, two or three feelings that they are going to 'specialise in'. These will persist over the next six months to four or five years, in varying intensity at various times. There are no *rules* about how we grieve. One of the reasons it is such a lonely and isolated place to be, is that it is so very different for each of us. One of the great mysteries of being human is that no one can ever *exactly* experience anyone else's grief. We can never get inside anyone else's skin, never *actually* go through it for them. How often we wish we could, especially when we see our children suffering!

After a long and painful illness, particularly if you have nursed or helped to look after someone, their death can bring a feeling of relief. Often you feel guilty that you are relieved. That is just something to pin the usual guilt associated with death on to. Of course you are relieved – for yourself and for the deceased. You may be exhausted physically and emotionally, have been through years of stress and physical strain, maybe great disruption to your family routine. If the deceased died after a long illness, you may have accompanied them from the beginning of that journey. You may have been their *anamchara*. You have been with them through diagnosis, tests, good and bad news, hopes dashed, moments of elation and despair, painful treatments or surgery, and then maybe slow and long-drawn-out wasting and deterioration. No wonder you are relieved! It does *not* mean you are glad they have died, *nor* does it mean you are selfish. After the initial relief, when you are physically and emotionally rested, you will feel the usual other feelings of grief.

Watching someone you love suffer is one of the hardest things life can bring, and of course the longer it goes on the harder it is. For many, death after such an illness is a 'happy release', and why not feel relief for them? Again you are not implying that they wanted to die, though of course some people do, and why not? As we all have to move on some time or other, do we not all hope for a time when we can accept death with *at least* equanimity, *at best* joy?

Summary

To summarise, here are some guidelines that can be useful when you first hear someone close has died:

- Take the usual measures for shock.
- Allow all the feelings to surface. Understand that it is quite normal to feel nothing, to be numb, or to disbelieve.
- Let the reality of the death sink in slowly. Use whatever tangible evidence you can, such as seeing the body or foetus, helping to lay them out, making arrangements for funeral and burial, telling people the news, and so on.
- Allow other feelings to surface as and when you become aware of them.
- Remember you are not alone, though it will feel as if you are. If you are physically alone, if possible go and talk to someone. If you don't have family or a friend you can talk to soon, there is usually someone – social worker, doctor, nurse, parish worker or clergy. You could talk to God, or whatever 'higher power' you believe in.

CHAPTER 2

DYING

Where Will it Be?

As a person approaches death, she may wish to make a decision about where she wants to die. Often when death is near we welcome the security and calm approach given by 'professionals' in a nursing home, hospital or hospice. Conversely, many people wish to return to, or remain at home, where they feel safer in more familiar surroundings.

Some of the issues that need to be looked at at this time are:

- We must respect the wishes of the dying person.
- We must listen to the advice of the doctors or consultants.
- We must consider the availability of help at home, for example, hospice homecare team, public-health nurses, Cancer Society and agency nurses. We must also consider their cost.
- We must consider other questions like the proximity of a hospital, hospice or nursing home, their visiting arrangements and so on.
- It is important to think about support for the family. It can be a daunting task for one person to be the sole carer in a remote area or in isolated circumstances.
- We should consider the effect on other family members.

Wishes of the dying person

It is important to ask the dying person what she would like. If you feel unable or awkward about asking, the doctor or nurse may ask her. It may not be possible to do what she wants, but it is much better to discuss it and tease out *why* it cannot be as she wishes, than for her to feel her wishes have not been considered.

Letting go of one's home is one the hardest of the 'letting gos', and deciding to die elsewhere often marks this task in a very definite way. If faced and worked through with a sympathetic loved one, or a professional, the dying person can be helped with this particular final goodbye to her home, one of many goodbyes. It allows her to have *some choice* in the goodbye at this time when, at best, so many choices are being made for her and, at worst, she may be treated as somewhat of an object. There is an enormous difference between saying goodbye with some choice, and feeling a complete victim of cruel circumstances.

Advice of doctors

This advice will usually be given after some discussion with the family and having taken the whole picture into consideration. Doctors will also have specialised knowledge of the pain control and other procedures and equipment that may be required in certain cases. Keeping someone at home can be made much easier by the support and co-operation of the doctor and nurse.

Availability of nursing care at home

If there is a hospice homecare team available, they provide tremendous support with nursing, pain control and other medical advice. Their very presence allows more free discussion in acknowledgement that the illness is terminal and death is approaching. Usually professional nursing care is needed in addition to the hospice homecare team as the illness progresses, and especially if the death is to be at home.

Some families are fortunate enough to have nurses who are family members, but pressure should not be put on them to do the nursing, even by way of unvoiced expectation. They may have their own job or family to care for, or it may be too difficult because of the family relationship.

If outside nursing care is required, there are usually various options, between public-health nurses, Cancer Society nurses, agency nurses and so on. Often family friends and neighbours help with less professionally skilled tasks, necessitating only a few hours of paid nursing. When care is required through the night, professional care is best, as family and those close can tire very quickly – after a day or two if they don't get enough rest. Various medical insurances can cover and contribute to home nursing costs, and some are free of charge, though these charities alone can seldom provide sufficient care.

If you have the money, this is not the time to stint on costs, and it is far more beneficial to the dying person, and usually the family too, than spending money on the wake or the funeral.

Other options

In larger cities there are usually a number of options if one chooses not to die at home. Even these options can be narrowed by availability of beds – which nowadays is a serious consideration – and by which hospitals the doctors concerned attend.

If the dying person is in a hospital, hospice or nursing home, and wishes to return to die in their own home, it deserves serious consideration from professionals, family and friends. It can sometimes be not only the fulfilment of a last dying wish, but a rewarding experience for all involved.

It often provides an opportunity to say all those things you never said, for all kinds of reasons – 'I love you', 'You've made a difference in my life', 'I forgive you', 'Do you forgive me?' Sometimes the intensity created by the circumstances can bring a closeness never before risked. There is an opportunity for planning the funeral, distributing possessions, planning for children's futures, and many other important issues. This can of course also be done in other settings, but the familiarity and informality of home make it easier.

Support for the family

Once again every family is different but, generally speaking, in the case of a long-drawn-out dying, 'big is beautiful'. Extended family, close friends and good neighbours can be invaluable. The more people there are to help, the less tired and strained everyone will be.

The very close person, the *anamchara* or 'death midwife', should try to get others to do the heavier physical work, cooking, cleaning, etc., so as they can keep their energy and attention for the dying person.

Don't be shy or afraid to ask for help. Most people consider it a compliment and are only waiting to be asked. Isn't that how you feel when someone asks for your help in such a situation?

Effect on other family members

This is particularly relevant when young children are involved, and in cases where there is another person needing a lot of attention as well as the one who is dying, for example an elderly or disabled person.

The decision as to whether small children should be 'protected' from the unpleasant side of illness and death, or allowed to learn from an early age that it is all part of life, is individual and depends on a number of factors. Children can learn fear from adults, and if the adults around them are not comfortable with a home death, the children will pick it up. Usually the adults' fear comes from early bad or fearful experiences with death and dying. If they can overcome it or find other less fearful people to help out, and a happy, natural atmosphere is created, children will not be hurt by whatever happens. Space must also be found for them to talk at length, and cry if they feel like it, about whatever is happening. This takes time and attention from at least one adult, a parent if possible.

I believe early familiarity, in a warm, secure atmosphere, with all that life can bring, is the best education and preparation for the many difficulties, losses and tragedies that we must all face.

I will deal at greater length with children's reaction to death in Chapter 9.

Regarding other family members, a lot depends on the availability of help and support, both physical and emotional. Nobody likes to feel they are a burden or a nuisance, either the dying person or other family members.

Questions

One of the greatest fears is fear of the unknown. For that reason, the dying person should be given as much information as they want (and no more). They should have all their questions taken seriously and answered. If you cannot answer them honestly, or if you haven't got sufficient knowledge to answer, find someone who can. Hospice staff or homecare teams are good at this. You can also ask the doctors involved, the public-health or other nurses, or knowledgeable friends.

Each person's fears are different, depending on their experience. I can only address some of the more common questions here. You must remember that questions are frequently asked from a need for reassurance, and often repeated over and over again. Be patient, reassure.

I have already dealt with the question of 'How long have I left?' People are less inclined to ask it close to the end, and seem to have more of a sense of it themselves then.

Will it be painful?

This is best answered in conjunction with professionals. Nowadays in the West, pain control has reached a considerable degree of sophistication, and it is rare that anyone has uncontrolled pain. You can say this quite truthfully, if asked.

It is very reassuring to say that you will do anything and everything you *can*, to ensure they will have as little pain as is humanly possible. Of course if you say that, you must be prepared to carry it out, which may mean standing firm with institutions or professionals. This can require a degree of courage and assertiveness.

Will you be there?

I have known many cases where a relative or friend has sat for days beside their dying loved one, and she has died while they went to the canteen for a quick cup of coffee, or to the bathroom. I believe that the dying person sometimes, somehow chooses this moment for the final breath, to save either themselves or those around them from what they perceive as the particular pain of that final moment.

However, the question is a good opening for you to find out whom the dying person would like to be present. So you can ask if they *would* like you to be there, and if they would like anyone else.

Elisabeth Kübler-Ross has a comforting belief that no one dies alone. She believes that the soul has the ability, at the moment of death, to go and be with whomsoever it wishes. This belief is also held by many ordinary people, some of whom claim to have experienced being 'visited' by a dying person to whom they were close.

As with all questions, be honest and sincere. Don't promise what you can't carry out. If you say you will do your very best, then be prepared to do just that.

The dying person may want to see a family member or loved one who lives far away before they die. They may wish such a person to be present when they die. I believe many people 'hold on' until a special person arrives, and then they let go and die quite peacefully. I have known this to happen in many cases.

So, if it is possible to bring people home from far away, when they are asked for, it can mean a lot to the dying person and make their passage easier and more contented.

Can I see a priest?

Two common reactions to this can be, a) 'Oh, no, you're not *that* ill', or b) 'Why? You haven't been to church for years!' These reactions can be explicitly spoken or just experienced inside us.

Hospitals and hospices usually look after blessings or anointing where that is traditional and when the dying person wishes it. But the dying person may wish to have a talk or confession with someone.

It is important always to comply with the request as soon as possible. The visit can and often does result in great healing (though not always physical healing or a 'cure'), and subsequent peace of mind.

Please let me die – now

Very occasionally and in unusual circumstances, a dying person can ask us to help them to 'end it all'. Fortunately, this is rarely a decision we have power to make, and in our culture it will be decided by the professionals. If the dying person asks you to tell the doctor, do so.

All I can say about it here is that when someone asks that, they do not *always* mean it. They are finding the situation they are in unbearable. We can help by alleviating their physical pain in practical ways, and their fear and emotional pain by listening and recommending, when we find it necessary, professional counselling or psychotherapy.

A Home Death

Many people are fearful of being with someone they love deeply at the moment of their death. A hospital chaplain once told me that he had been with many hundreds of people when they died and almost all had died peacefully.

If it is a home death, you can spend those last precious days and hours together, or with family members, in a way you will remember after the acute pain of loss has diminished, as a beautiful, tender, loving and enriching time.

As I have said, it is important that the dying person's physical needs are attended to first, including pain relief. This is no small task and takes up a lot of time. It is not an entirely separate task, of course, from the emotional and spiritual care, and all can be combined.

Depending on the situation, all the family and very many close friends and relatives can be involved in various ways. Usually, each finds their own level, the way in which *they* can best contribute.

One of the most valuable people is the one who sits quietly and holds the dying person's hand. While she is still conscious you can, and should, ask her what she wants.

At this point I would like to tell you the story of a wonderful woman who took her mother home to die.

Anna decided to bring her mother Nora home when she was thought to have a few weeks left to live, as she had advanced secondary cancer of the stomach. She decided on a Friday, and it was the Monday before she had it organised sufficiently and her mother came home. She discussed it with the consultant in the hospital and her own doctor first, and both agreed it was a good idea.

She reorganised her mother's house. She moved Nora's bed down to the living room and rearranged it for nursing. She left space all around the bed for carers to walk, moved some of the furniture out, and put in a comfortable chair for her to sit in, or even to doze in at night.

As it was likely that her mother would probably only live for three or four weeks at the very most, Anna decided to take on a good deal of the caring herself. She realised she would not be able to do it on her own, so she organised two people to help her alternately. Her family would be there in the evenings. At first Nora slept through the night and Anna slept in the next room.

As soon as Nora was home, Anna got in touch with the local public-health nurse, who called daily.

She contacted the local hospice after a week, where she got advice on how to control her mother's constipation and, as Nora got weaker, the hospice nurse from the homecare team came every day.

During the last few days the nurse put a pump in one of Nora's veins so Nora could have morphine without the discomfort of oral tablets, suppositories or injections. This is a simple procedure.

That was the practical side and was so important. Elisabeth Kübler-Ross says that a person *must* be physically comfortable and out of pain before they can deal with mental and emotional issues surrounding death and dying.

Anna had never had a good relationship with her mother. She, as an only girl, was her father's 'pet'. Her mother favoured the boys. Anna's father had died two years earlier and Anna had grieved him very thoroughly. She had allowed all the feelings to surface and expressed them with a number of close friends and a therapist. She had, I would say, fully completed the four 'tasks of grieving' (see Introduction).

Lately, before her mother became ill, Anna had decided to work in therapy on the relationship with her mother. It had been difficult at times, and painful too, but after some months she began to realise that, buried underneath all her anger and disappointment with her mother, there was a lot of love. The therapy allowed her to uncover this love and to let it blossom. When her mother became ill, she was able to listen to her better than previously, but she still found it difficult. She continued with her therapy.

When she brought her mother home she experienced two amazing weeks. Almost miraculously, but actually due to a lot of hard work, she was able to care physically for her mother in a most loving and tender way. She was also able to support her emotionally and converse with her in ways that healed their relationship and helped her mother to die. Anna sat for hours and held her mother's hand. She massaged her body, stroked her face. She washed her and fed her, all with deep love and tenderness. She told her Mum how much she loved her, and her Mum replied that she loved her too.

Nora asked Anna if she had been a good mother; she said that it worried her. Anna, always straight and truthful said, 'You just have to look at us – haven't we turned out well?' (which they had), and her Mum smiled and said, 'Yes, and *you* are wonderful.' They both cried together.

Her Mum talked a lot about going home, and one day said 'Anna, you know I have to go. I'm sorry, I'm sorry.' Anna said, 'I know, and it's okay for you to go. I'm sorry too. I'll miss you. But we'll be together, spiritually', and her Mum nodded. She seemed at peace.

Anna was conscious much of the time with her Mum, in those last weeks, of a special presence in the room. Her mother frequently talked aloud to John (her deceased husband, Anna's father) and sometimes to others. Many people believe that those close to us, who have already died, come to visit, to be with us, when our turn comes. I have heard many times of dying people experiencing this. Several times in the last week Nora became very weak and Anna felt she was going, but she revived for a day, or a few hours, and was cheerful and joked with everyone. On her last morning, she was conscious. Nora told Anna, 'I love you, I love you, I love you, and I could never tell you,' and Anna replied, 'And I love you too, so much, and I could never tell you either.' They hugged and held each other. Nora said, 'I'm off to a party!' What a wonderful description of heaven! That afternoon Nora quietly slipped into a coma which became deeper, until she died very peacefully, with all the family and her carers around her, at 5 a.m. the next morning, two weeks after she had come home. Anna helped to lay her out. They kept her at home so that friends could come and sympathise and say goodbye.

Naturally, all home deaths cannot be like Nora's, but I feel it is important to be aware of how it *can* be done. What was different in this situation was the short time Nora was seriously ill. Anna could never have kept up the kind of care and attention she gave her mother for more than a few weeks. Secondly, Anna had no ties or responsibilities herself that could not be shelved for a short period, and that too is unusual.

However, Anna told me that she would have done anything possible to have had this time, and quality of time, with her Mum. She said that she felt she could get money any time in her life, but she could never have those last days of her mother's life again. She said that up to then, she had plodded along, taking every day for granted. While caring for her mother, each day was one closer to her death, and each morning, on waking, Anna would think, 'Maybe she will only have this day left. I must make this one special.' It has helped her to live this way even after her mother's death, to appreciate the gift of each day as it comes.

It is most people's (though not everyone's) wish to die at home in their own beds. If it can be managed, it is a wonderful gift both for the dying person and all those involved.

Our Own Fears

As I described in the last chapter, most of our fears about death and dying can be traced back to either our past bad experiences or fear of our own dying.

Fear traditionally brings about 'fight or flight'. In humans, this can look like *taking control* (fight) or *avoidance* (flight). They are two opposite ends of the same pattern of behaviour, which is acted on in order to reduce the level of our pain, fear, anxiety, etc.

What is important here is how these fears of our own are affecting the dying person with whom we are journeying. If you are experiencing any of the following, perhaps you need to look at and deal with those fears.

Taking control

The more we can control what is happening, the less we are afraid. When someone is dying we must be careful not to let our fears dictate what happens. What *she*, the dying person, wants is what we must respect.

You may find yourself becoming 'bossy' and 'busy-busy', that is, taking control of the household or the illness, *beyond what your role dictates*, and to the diminishment of whatever power and control the ill person can still take. If so, the reason is most likely to be your own pain or fear. If you find yourself making decisions without consulting either the ill person, if it is appropriate, or other members of the family, stop and think.

Of course, when the dying person expresses her wishes to you and you act as an advocate or intermediary, or as her voice or spokesperson, that is a different matter. It is all a question of constantly checking your motives.

Avoidance

There is something of the 'if I don't think about it, it will go away' about avoidance!

Do you find yourself staying away from your loved one or staying out of the 'sick room'? Do you avoid certain subjects when you are with her, for example, deep feelings about love, unfinished business, and death? Do you manipulate the conversation to avoid these subjects?

Of course, life is about living in the present, even when you are dying. The deeper and more painful subjects, such as these, are not to be talked about every day. For some dying people it is just too much and they never address them, at least directly, but *they should be given every chance*. It is their life and their death, and they should be allowed to choose. It is all about balance. Left enough space and freedom, they will get it right for themselves.

You can deal with your own hurts about past experiences, and fears about your own mortality and dying, as recommended in Chapter 14.

Counselling and Psychotherapy

If you think the dying person needs professional counselling or psychotherapy, first of all check with them if that is what they want. There are a number of reasons why someone who is dying may need professional help of this kind. Family or friends are either too close, not available, not willing, or too shy, embarrassed or upset. For these reasons, the simplicity of employing someone to whom we owe nothing, except cash, can be relieving and refreshing at a time when there is much emotion around.

Maybe asking the dying person can be enough of a push for her to open up and to talk to you. She may no longer need a counsellor then. *Telling* someone they *need* counselling is the surest way to put them off!

It does not mean, of course, that the dying person will not also talk to you or others. She may even talk more as a result.

Finding a counsellor or therapist

For the purpose of this book I will use the words 'counselling' and 'psychotherapy' (or therapy) to mean the same thing although, in my opinion, there is some difference.

Finding a suitable counsellor or therapist outside of big cities is largely dependent on availability. If you have no personal contacts or recommendations, get in touch with your doctor, nurse or social worker, or one of the professional counselling or psychotherapy bodies. There are often counsellors or therapists attached to hospitals, or they can recommend one.

Depending on the therapist, she may ask all the family to see her together, maybe even with the dying person. Or she may see the family without the dying person for a separate session – or see the dying person and her partner.

All this is usually suggested to help the whole family, or all those involved, to address 'unfinished business' and maybe to say their goodbyes. These very difficult tasks can often be made less painful by having a 'stranger' present, who is a little outside the strong emotions that dying can evoke.

If the dying person is in a hospice or hospital ward, she may wish to see a therapist not connected with the hospice or hospital. If this is the case, check first, and arrange it with the ward sister or whoever is in charge. She may suggest contacting the hospital or hospice social worker. In this way some privacy can usually be organised for the visit. Therapists do not work miracles; they can only make a contribution to a very painful situation.

Settling Affairs

Planning a will

If your dying friend or loved one asks you if you think she should make a will, you may be tempted in your embarrassment or sorrow to advise them not to bother, or to postpone it. This may be because *you* want to deny that they are dying, or because you don't want *them* to realise it in such a concrete way. Making a will is better done when we are in full health, but if it has not been attended to previously, it should not be delayed.

If you feel it is appropriate, it can be most helpful to enquire if she has already made a will and, if not, to suggest it.

Sometimes people wish to give away small personal items such as jewellery. It can be an enriching experience to give these away while one is still relatively well. Again, it is a powerful feeling to be able actually to dispose of one's most precious possessions to people who are special to us in our lives. Some solicitors advise including all items in a will, while others suggest leaving a separate letter of instructions for the executor.

You may be asked to be an executor of the will, and before agreeing it is useful to know what this entails. Basically, you are acting, in the deceased's absence, for her, to ensure her wishes are carried out as laid down in the will. If a solicitor is involved, and there is money in the estate to pay her, it does not entail a great deal of work on your part, unless it is a complicated will or it is contested. Having a solicitor as one executor does make it a lot easier. If the will is contested, this could involve a lot more time and work. It also can mean becoming involved in a lot of family unpleasantness, which can be even worse if you yourself are a family member. If one of the executors is a solicitor, she can often, as an outsider, more easily deal with family disagreements. In the case of the will being contested, you will not be personally financially liable.

It is possible to make a will without having a solicitor. It must be dated and witnessed by two people who are not beneficiaries. It should be kept in a safe place and the executor or a family member should be told of its existence and whereabouts. Forms for this purpose are available from larger stationery outlets.

It is also possible for an executor to execute an estate without using a solicitor. It is an extremely time-consuming task, unless it is a very straight-forward will, but it costs no more than probate office fees, which are charged on a sliding scale relative to the value of the estate.

Solicitors also charge on a sliding scale relative to the value of the estate. Their fees will, of course, be for their time and services, which you are saved if you execute it yourself.

Funeral Arrangements

Some people draw a lot of comfort from being able to make known their wishes for their own funeral and burial or cremation. The degree of detail in which they wish to become involved varies from person to person. Helping a dying person to plan their own funeral can be a difficult thing to do, but like many of these tasks of letting go, it can be rewarding and give a feeling of peace and completion, both to you and the dying person.

A lot of listening is required to give the dying person space to be creative and to express what she really wants, not what she feels she *ought* to do. Don't come in too soon with suggestions, unless she is finding it very difficult. If you do, make sure it is a *suggestion only*, and perhaps it can be a stimulus to spark off more ideas.

The kind of ritual you can create depends to a large extent on which religion, if any, the person belongs to. Many people like to have the traditional ritual of the religion they grew up with, even though they may no longer be practising that religion. Most religions will allow that. If in doubt, ask the minister concerned. Most religions have some parameters within which they require you to work.

I will deal with the different rituals that mark dying, death and committal, both traditional and unconventional, in Chapter 12. I will discuss input into traditional rituals and the creation of new rituals.

Cremation or burial

Nowadays more and more people wish to be cremated. Funeral directors will arrange this just as simply as burials, except that not every city or town has a crematorium, so it may entail travelling quite a long distance in some cases.

If the dying person expresses a wish to be cremated, or wishes to discuss it, be careful not to let your own unfamiliarity with it put her off what she really wants.

Organ donation

If it has been discussed before death, and the family are aware that organs are to be donated, this can be done very simply. The Kidney Association usually prints cards for prospective donors to carry, with specific instructions. These cards are not legally binding. The family or next of kin make the actual decision. Of course the vast majority go along with the deceased person's wishes.

Organs can only be used when death has occurred in hospital and the person has been alive on a ventilator while brain dead. The exception to this is the donation of eyes. Further information can be obtained from the relevant agencies.

Organ donation does not hold up the time of the funeral.

Body donation

People wishing to donate their bodies for medical research should contact their GP or their local university medical school's department of anatomy. The department will clarify all the various issues that arise in these cases.

CHAPTER 3

DEATH

Attitudes, Beliefs and Viewpoints

Reacting as whole people

I look on human beings as whole organisms, made up of components – body, mind, emotions and spirit – which interact in an extremely complex manner. In this context, what we believe – our attitude to or viewpoint on death, dying, and the question and quality of life after death – influences our emotions, which in turn affects our bodies, our spiritual life, and therefore how we grieve. If we give equal weight or importance to each part of our make-up, we recognise the effect each one has on the others, but we do not ignore any component. If we do, we may do so at our own peril, to the detriment of our health, physical, mental, emotional and spiritual.

So even if we have a very 'positive' belief about what happens to us after death, it does not entirely block out all 'negative' emotions about the loss. It does not stop our feeling sad and grieving.

A 'positive' view of death or life hereafter can certainly be of immense comfort, and ease the pain of loss. It should not be used as part of denial, as an excuse not to feel the emotional pain of the loss.

In our mainly Christian culture, we receive mixed messages about death. I believe that these mixed *messages* are a projection and rationalisation of the mixed *feelings* we do indeed have about death, both positive and negative. It is difficult to have a clear, rational view of death. If you have a clear view, that is fine. If you do not, that is also fine. Most of life is neither black nor white, good nor bad, positive nor negative. Much of it is grey, a mixture, with occasional patches of black and white.

The moment of death is, I believe, the greatest reminder we ever get that we humans are not in absolute control, not the all-powerful 'masters of the universe' we might allow ourselves to pretend we are. Not in the egotistical way we see it, anyway.

Death, therefore, can evoke feelings of deep terror of an instinctual nature, threatening our very existence. And yet, paradoxically, when we are with a loved one who dies peacefully (as the majority of people in our society at present do) we are, frequently, in spite of the grief, somehow strangely reassured as to the naturalness of this point of transition. We may be able to see how peaceful a moment it can be in those situations. But that does not negate our own feelings of threat, fear and loss.

Shock, numbness, denial, isolation

As I have explained previously, in order to cope and survive, we cannot allow ourselves to feel immediately the enormity of what has happened when someone we love dies. The fact that these feelings come in stages is not only natural and usual, but useful, maybe essential, for many people.

The *shock* will have the same effect as any severe physical shock, and you can expect mainly physical signs or symptoms. If you know what to expect, you will not be too taken aback. Shock can persist from minutes to weeks after a death. It is quite usual to experience shock even if the deceased had been terminally ill for years, or dying for some time. If the death has been sudden or violent, in an accident or suicide, the shock may be greater, and may persist for longer. One of the reasons for this is that the bereaved person has done absolutely no grieving beforehand. Anticipatory grieving is believed to help people grieve afterwards, though it does not replace it. The quality of anticipatory grieving is quite different.

Numbness in this context is not meant to describe a physical feeling (or lack of feeling), but it can sometimes be experienced physically. People feel dazed and unreal, as if they are in a bad dream. Even if they try to realise at any deep level, or feel what has happened, they are not able to, initially.

Denial is partly rationalisation of the numbness. If I can't feel or realise this has happened, then *it has not happened!* Denial and numbness work together effectively to keep out the full realisation, and help us cope.

Denial is the first 'stage' mentioned by Elisabeth Kübler-Ross. It has many manifestations and can be confusing for the bereaved, and confusing and extremely irritating for those around her.

At this stage, it is common to believe that you see the dead person in a street or crowd. Often the bereaved person will run after them, only to be shocked and disappointed when she realises she is mistaken. If you do this you are not going mad! It is perfectly normal. This phase will pass, though isolated incidents can still happen for years after the death. Similarly, we can fantasise about seeing the deceased or hearing them.

As a child, after my father died, I made up a lovely story that one day, on my way home from school, I would get on the bus and my Daddy would be sitting there. We'd hug and talk and go home together, and my Mum would be delighted that I had brought him home.

Years later, my mother told me she would often think it was my father when the phone rang during the day. He had often rung her from his work. Or when it was the time he used to come home in the evenings, she used to imagine she heard his keys in the door.

Silence is one of the hardest things – never to hear the beloved voice again.

> Oh for the touch of a vanished hand,
> And the sound of a voice that is still. *(Thomas Moore)*

These visual and other types of images can be quite painful when we are jolted back into reality. They are part of yearning for the deceased, a feeling often experienced early on in the grieving process. Yearning often takes the form of a physical pain, usually in the chest or stomach. If such pains are severe or persist, consult your doctor.

Some doctors prescribe drugs, especially in the first days, or even for weeks after a death. If they are prescribed for a specific medical condition, that is of course a matter for your doctor. If not, and you simply want to deaden the pain, maybe try to get through without them, or without much alcohol or smoking. It will feel worse at the time, but the grieving process, which is a natural one, will have begun. The longer you postpone it, the more difficult it will be.

Sometimes some light medication can help you to sleep through those first difficult nights. If you really need this, you can ask your doctor for something that will not inhibit your grieving.

Isolation often takes the form of experiencing the world around as if through a pane of glass, cut off from you. In some way, this increases the sense that you are alone in this terrible moment of crisis, and that no one can possibly understand. Even if some people close to you can understand, it is of little or no help at this point, as you are unable to 'let them in'. But try not to drive them away, as you may be tempted to do, perhaps in despair. Their very presence is better than total isolation, and they can perform all sorts of useful practical tasks which allow you to focus on the initial phase or stage of grieving, without distraction.

Denial and reality

The more involved you can become in the reality of the death, the better and easier your grieving will be. Neither life, nor death, are ever perfect or ideal; you can only do your best. If you can participate in some, or even any, of the events surrounding the dying, death and funeral rites, it will help greatly afterwards. It may feel very difficult and painful at the time, though not necessarily.

If you can participate in some of the following ways, it should help:

- Any caring that can be done before the death.
- Be present when the person dies.
- Lay her out or help with it.
- Communicate with funeral directors, clergy, family members and close friends, graveyard or cremation personnel.
- Become involved in planning the funeral and burial or cremation rituals.
- Participate in these rituals.
- Tidy up and, if appropriate, distribute the deceased's belongings.
- Deal with solicitors or legal officials regarding the will and distribution of the estate.
- Become involved in the production of obituaries, memorials, headstones, engraving, etc.

It is seldom possible to be involved in all of these, but often more possible, and nowadays more common, than you may think. Children can be included in all but a few events and, if in doubt, it is more important for them not to be excluded. This will be dealt with further in Chapter 9. If you are the next of kin or closest person, and you are not stepping on anyone's toes, push yourself just a little further than you might have done previously to be involved.

Deaths are often times of great family splits and disputes; often too, times of great reconciliation. I am not suggesting you ever get involved to the exclusion of anyone else.

Euphoria

Some people experience a kind of elation, sometimes called 'euphoria', with the feelings of numbness and denial. It is most common in the first few days or weeks. It can be truly positive in helping with 'getting through' that really difficult time. You may experience a rather feverish spurt of energy for such tiring tasks as house cleaning. It is important not to allow yourself to become too exhausted at this time when you need your energy for tiring ceremonies and the emotions of grieving, or even for entertaining relatives or commiserating friends and neighbours.

Sudden death

Like any death, sudden death has its own particular pain and problems. It also has some compensations. As mentioned above, the lack of anticipatory grieving, of warning, leaves the shock totally uncushioned. I believe the physical feelings of shock are often more pronounced with sudden death. The early reaction of denial is often stronger. The involvement in the realities as mentioned above are, therefore, even more important.

In practical terms, there is more disruption, even chaos, usually while the bereaved person is in strong denial or shock. This increases the feeling of threat to the ground of security and the feelings of fear and dread.

Because you are even more deeply shocked, and the practicalities are even more difficult to deal with, you may need more help and support from friends or professionals in the case of a sudden death. Allow yourself to be helped and supported. If you need more, ask for it. It is usually more difficult to receive than to give. Be humble – there is a time for all of us.

Many sudden deaths are violent and I will deal with this separately in Chapter 7.

Relief

It is much more common than you think to feel relieved after a death. You are not the only one, if you are feeling this way.

The most common feeling is relief for the person who has died after a long or painful illness. In that case, you can be relieved that you do not have to carry the strain or responsibility of nursing any longer. If you have been worried or anxious about, for example, an elderly person living alone, it can be a relief to know nothing can happen to them ever again. You can be relieved too if there was a difficult relationship between you and the deceased, or between her and others. When the deceased was a very unhappy person, maybe deeply depressed, or torn with mental anguish, you can also feel relieved.

These feelings of relief are natural and should never cause guilt. However, guilt is a very common feeling during grieving, and should be acknowledged, expressed, understood and integrated. It does not mean you were in any way at fault or to blame. It is felt alongside deep sorrow and in no way negates your sorrow at your loss.

If the deceased has left specific wishes for her funeral and burial or cremation, it is usually most comforting to those left behind to carry out these wishes as closely as possible. One of the reasons we hold such rituals is to honour the person who has died and her memory. Doing it the way she wanted it to be, is part of that respect and honouring.

If the deceased has not left any instructions, you have a choice. You can do it as you imagine they would have wanted it, or do it as you would like it. In my experience, what works best is a mixture of both. These rituals are, after all, for the living as well as the dead.

As I have said, death and bereavement evoke all kinds of feelings of powerlessness. So any way you can take charge of things helps to counteract those feelings. Funeral directors are a really useful resource at this time. Use them as such. They will be delighted to take the time to describe all the options you have regarding the following:

Death notices – where they should be placed, how they should be worded. People are becoming much more creative lately, and I see some notices now mention close friends as well as family. They also often include other very personal pieces specific to that particular person or to the circumstances of death.

What clothes or habit the person should be laid out in, and if they should be made up. In situations where there have been head injuries, or the body has been mutilated in some way, this may be necessary. The funeral directors will advise.

Where the person is to be laid out or waked. In some countries people are laid out at home rather than in a morgue or funeral parlour, especially when they have died at home. On occasion, people are even brought home from a hospital or funeral home for this very personal family way of saying goodbye.

Type of coffin and decorations on it. Remember, expensive isn't necessarily beautiful! Don't make the mistake of trying to make up now for omissions during the deceased's lifetime, by giving her a 'good send off'. In spite of popular belief, it is not necessary to have handles on a coffin to help it to be lowered into the ground. This can be done easily by using straps.

The Memorial Service varies, first of all, according to the religion and who is conducting the ceremony. Within that variation there are many choices. These include choice of readings, music, hymns, who can and should participate, and the nature of that participation.

You can use the funeral director as an intermediary here or you can plan it yourself with whoever is involved.

Flowers. You can specify in the death notice if you want flowers or not, and if you want cut flowers only. The funeral directors can order flowers on your behalf if you wish. Afterwards, some people like to give the fresh flowers to a hospital or local nursing home, maybe where the person died. Some people give them to various relatives for their homes. Another idea is to put some on nearby graves of relatives and friends.

Flowers for decorating the church. This can be done professionally or by family and friends.

Music can be played, or hymns or special songs sung by a professional or by family and friends. You can have a variety of types of music if you wish, in consultation of course with whoever is leading the ceremony.

Funeral cars can be provided by the funeral directors. It is much less stressful not to have to worry about driving, traffic and parking, when you are grieving. However, you may prefer to have a friend drive you in their car or your own car.

Committal. Different decisions and arrangements have to be made depending on whether the remains are to be buried or cremated. In Chapter 12, I will deal in more detail with various rituals you can create yourself or help to create, or how you can help shape and participate in the more conventional funeral services.

PART II

EXPERIENCING THE PAIN

CHAPTER 4

GRIEVING: THE EARLY DAYS

How Long Will I Feel This Bad?

It is when the numbness begins to 'thaw' and reality begins to sink in that is probably the hardest time of all for the bereaved person. This can happen anytime from hours to about three months after the death.

When you begin to feel, the most important thing to remember is that feeling is fine. Allow the feelings to surface, no matter how unpleasant they are. Do not avoid any of the feelings or suppress them with alcohol or drugs. If possible, try not to suppress them with milder 'drugs' either, such as cigarettes, food, tea, coffee or sex – or whatever you use to suppress your feelings.

One fairly common irrational way of suppressing feelings of early grief is to try to replace the deceased immediately with someone else to relate to in a similar way. This can prove dangerous if the deceased was a spouse, partner, lover, or if it was any type of 'romantic relationship'. You may find yourself having romantic or sexual feelings for someone who is close and caring to you at this point. This is quite normal, but making any decision about that relationship at this time is not to be advised. In fact, never make any major decision about any part of your life for about a year after a very close bereavement.

This also applies to 'replacing' children who have died – especially before birth or at a very young age – by having another baby. I will deal with that further in Chapter 13.

All kinds of feelings can surface. Unless you act irrationally on them, or they prevent you eating or sleeping over a period, it is normal and usual. You are not going mad, even if thoughts of suicide cross your mind. Of course if these persist, or you are really planning to kill yourself, please seek help.

Yes, life has changed utterly. It will certainly never be the same again. There are long sad days ahead, difficult weeks, months, probably years, to come. But the grief will slowly diminish, the acuteness of the pain will fade. The physical pain fades first, and, much later, and more slowly, the emotional pain.

Physical symptoms

Some people express their pain emotionally, that is through their feelings. Some people 'somatise' their grief, that is, their bodies express it. Most people do a bit of both. You may find you have all sorts of strange unexplained pains and aches in the early stages of grieving. This is quite usual. If they persist or are of a serious nature, consult your doctor.

In the first year after losing a spouse, studies have shown that people visit the doctor a lot more often. They are somewhat more likely to contract a serious illness or die themselves.

Timing

It is almost impossible to predict how long anyone will continue to grieve. No matter what anyone tells you, there is no such thing as normal! I believe there are five stages in the intensity of grieving:

1. Feeling terrible all the time, and it feels unbearable.
2. Feeling terrible all the time and it feels bearable.
3. Feeling bad with periods when you can forget, but when you 'remember' the pain, it seems worse.
4. Forgetting for periods, and this helps you to bear the feeling when you 'remember' the pain. Sometimes enjoying yourself again.
5. The fifth stage expands until you can enjoy life as much (or even more) than before the death. I will deal further with this in Chapter 14.

Work

In our society, the traditional period given for grieving (by employers) is three days. Many people are unable to return to work after this short time. This is quite usual. If you feel unable to work and need a doctor's certificate, ask your doctor. If you work at home, ask friends, neighbours and relatives to help.

Nobody should be expected to 'pull themselves together' after three days. This is a particularly short time if a) they are physically exhausted for various reasons, or b) the death was sudden or violent and they are still in shock to some degree.

But how long?

As it is so difficult to put a time on the grieving period, in doing so I run the risk of whatever I say being 'used', often against the bereaved person. Relatives and friends, tired of listening, exasperated or irritated because of their own unresolved grief, often quote various sources as to how long grieving *ought* to last. However, I would say that in grieving the death of a partner, spouse, lover, close friend, parent, child or sibling, or other significant person, taking four years to *complete* the process is quite usual.

If you have been recently bereaved, do not let this depress you. You may begin to see four lonely desperate years ahead. It is not like that.

Remember the five stages (above). These four years are not four years *out* of your life but an important part *of* your life. Your daily routine may continue, or a new one emerge during this time. Much learning and emotional and spiritual growth can take place. Children grow and develop new friendships, new interests are developed, babies are born, even other people die.

It can be a real *turning point* in your life (see Introduction).

CHAPTER 5

GRIEVING CONTINUES

Anniversaries

The anniversary of a death means a year after the death, but to me it has more than a day as well. An anniversary is a marking of any period of time since the death occurred. Therefore twenty-four hours after the death occurred is a type of anniversary; it reminds us of the day "this time yesterday she was still alive". All these "anniversaries" bring back pain of a particular kind of way. Then you have the weekly, the monthly, the yearly anniversaries.

Many people are conscious of all kinds of anniversaries surrounding terminal illness and death: the anniversaries of the onset of the illness, diagnosis, hospitalization, remission, and so on. Then there are anniversaries of the causes of death, such as accidents, murders, bomb attacks, if the person died later as a result of something like that. There are anniversaries of the funeral and other rituals. All in all, there are many occasions when one is poignantly reminded of what has happened, through the meaning and passing of time.

You can look on these as painful reminders, or as special days. You can mark them in many ways, from simple marking the occasion privately, to holding rituals or family gatherings. The Christian Churches, and the Roman Catholic Church in particular, sometimes have Mass or services held to mark some of these occasions. We tend to learn how heavily on anniversaries is our own individual way of coping, and should be able to mark them in a way and at a level that is our own.

If you are very conscious of these anniversaries of your loved one's death, and find it lonely and sad to cope, maybe you should mark some of these times by gathering people together, for a meal or ritual. Maybe you should visit the grave, light a candle, and of them who, or simply spend a quiet time thinking about your loved one, praying or meditating. I will find more on this in the next chapter or ritual.

CHAPTER 5

GRIEVING CONTINUES

Anniversaries

The anniversary of a death means a year after the death, but to me it means more than that as well. An anniversary is a marking of any period of time since the death occurred. Therefore twenty-four hours after the death occurred is a type of anniversary. It reminds us of the death: 'This time yesterday she was still alive'. All these 'anniversaries' bring back pain in a particular kind of way. Then you have the weekly, the monthly, the yearly anniversaries.

Some people are conscious of all kinds of anniversaries surrounding terminal illness and death: the anniversary of the onset of the illness, diagnosis, hospitalisation, recurrence, and so on. Then there are anniversaries of the causes of death, such as accidents, murders, bomb attacks, if the person died later as a result of something like that. There are anniversaries of the funerals and other rituals. All in all, there are many occasions when we are poignantly reminded of what has happened, through the marking and passing of time.

You can look on these as painful reminders, or as special times. You can mark them in many ways, from simply noting the occasion privately, to holding rituals or family gatherings. The Christian Churches, and the Roman Catholic Church in particular, sometimes have Mass or services held to mark some of these occasions. We tend to lean too heavily on institutions to provide us with ritual. We can create our own – and should. We do, of course, create some, often without being aware of it (see Chapter 12).

If you are very conscious of those anniversaries of your loved one's death, and find it lonely, tell someone. Maybe you should mark some of these times by gathering people together for a meal or ritual. Maybe you should visit the grave, visit a relative and tell them why, or simply spend a little quiet time thinking about your loved one, praying or meditating. I will deal more with this in the chapter on ritual.

Firsts

The first time you do something without your loved one can be painful and lonely, sometimes so difficult that you may avoid certain occasions or doing certain things. There are many, and each of you will know the ones that are particularly painful, for example, the first time you go to church without her, the first visit to your special place like a restaurant, weekly shopping, a walk in the country, or holidays. The pain you experience at these times can be acute. Try asking someone to go with you. Then you can use some of the time to talk about the good times you had together there, and maybe even to cry. This is an important part of grieving. Do not go with someone and pretend to be having a great time or that the past never happened. Do not wait for months. Go to some of the places quite soon with someone close, and grieve. The 'first' feeling will be over. It will never be quite so painful again.

There are also 'firsts' associated with the death itself, like the first time you go back to the place where your loved one died, and this is extremely difficult if they died violently, in an accident, bomb attack or similar event. Even more important is to find someone sensitive and understanding to accompany you.

The first birthdays can be lonely, yours and theirs, especially if birthdays were big events in your lives. Special family-type occasions can be agonising and isolating. If it is a partner you have lost, and other people there have their partners with them, you can feel extremely bereft. There are so many of these occasions: christenings; first communions; confirmations; weddings; funerals; conferring of degrees; and, worst of all for most people, Christmas and New Year.

Christmas

Christmas, and the first Christmas especially, can be nothing short of a nightmare for many bereaved people. Christmas has become a travesty of what it is supposed to represent in our society. This becomes painfully evident to anyone who has experienced a Christmas when grieving a loved one. From that depth of sorrow it is even easier to see the falseness and hypocrisy of the commercialisation of it all.

Most families have their own particular Christmas traditions. The other members usually expect you, the bereaved, to join in the festivities or usual celebrations. If you think this would help you, or if you feel it would be less painful and less lonely than other options, that is fine. If, however, you feel you would be genuinely happier spending at least some of it on your own, or doing something quite different, do what *you* want to do.

Here are some examples:

- If your husband has died, and you always spent family Christmases with his family in their houses, you might stay in your home and create your own family Christmas with your children, and possibly other family members or friends.
- If you don't feel like spending the whole day with the family, spend only a part of it with them. Have a little private quiet time at home, alone for part of the day, or go for a walk in the mountains, or go and visit a different family or friend, perhaps a lonely one.
- If you are single and alone, invite or join someone in a similar position. If you can afford it, go for a holiday, visit long lost relations in Australia, go skiing or visit friends.

A warning: If you go away from home, you postpone some aspects of the 'first Christmas' without your loved one. One day you will probably have to face it. However, in a year or two, you will be stronger and find it somewhat easier.

What Can You Do?

- Mark the occasion. Do not let it go unnoticed. Mark the absence of the deceased.
- Use all these occasions to remember times past, always including the good memories.
- Try not to endure them all on your own. Ask people to join you. They could be lonely too. Most people would be flattered – wouldn't you?
- Create rituals to mark the occasions. They may be simple or

elaborate, they may be your own, family or institutional rituals.
- Plan ahead, even if you are planning a quiet time alone with your thoughts and memories. Decide how long you will spend on this 'special' time.
- Do it your way. Don't get pulled into joining in on occasions you do not wish to be part of. Do not be afraid to stand out, be different, even to be absent.

Visiting the Grave

Some individuals make a ritual of visiting the grave. Many find it comforting, using the visit as a time to grieve, or a way of remembering or honouring the deceased. It is common to visit frequently during the first few months, and some people visit weekly for a year or more. Some people use tending the grave as a symbolic way of caring for the deceased, and showing they have not forgotten. Some communities, especially in rural Ireland, have customs of decorating graves, and in most Irish Roman Catholic parishes there is a 'Cemetery Sunday' each year, when a Mass is said in the graveyard. Numbers of people turn out for this ceremony, and many decorate graves beautifully for the occasion. If this idea appeals to you, participate in it. Group rituals like that can engender a warm feeling of community spirit and support.

As I have said, visiting the grave can be a comforting and therapeutic exercise and a way of remembering and honouring the dead. It can also become a way of staying stuck in a type of denial. If so, you may be using it as a way of saying to yourself that your loved one may have died, but is still here. In this way you can visit and communicate with them anytime you wish. Thus, you can avoid acknowledging the stark reality of death – that the whole person you knew and loved has gone. If you feel drawn to visiting too often, or staying too long at the grave, wean yourself away by cutting down slowly. Set up a quiet 'special' room in your house, and visit it instead. If it is a room, gradually reduce this 'shrine' to a corner of the room, then maybe a photograph. Develop a place of communion with the deceased in your *heart*, where it will remain for as long as you want.

Disposal of Ashes

Some people leave instructions in their will for the disposal of their ashes. These instructions can be detailed. If the instructions are simply where to scatter the ashes, you may wish to make a ritual of the event. If the ashes are to be buried, you could invite a priest or similar person to conduct the ritual. The funeral director can deliver the ashes and organise the grave-digger if you wish. Whatever type of ritual you plan, invite people to join you who are significant to you, as well as to the deceased.

This also can be an important and satisfying part of grieving, as you are often disposing of your loved one's remains in a manner and place that was significant and special to them, often a place they really loved. This engenders a feeling of still being able to do something for them, and at this stage there is not much else that can give you this feeling.

Getting on With Life While Actively Grieving

As early as weeks after the death, you can be sure some friends will be suggesting that you 'pull yourself together'! No matter how well intentioned, they probably mean by this that they are finding it difficult to see you still hurting. This reaction is nothing more selfish than that their own pain is being re-stimulated, by seeing you in pain. If they have had to 'pull themselves together' too soon after someone close to *them* died, they will find the pain of having had to do that being re-stimulated, when they see you not 'pulling yourself together'. It is a vicious circle!

However, there is some good sense in getting your attention away from grieving for short periods of the day, after three or four weeks. It does not mean your attention will go away from the loss, but from actively grieving. Choose to do this in whatever way you wish, not to please your family or friends. You cannot be expected to go to parties or occasions where people are in 'hilarious' mood. Go to visit a few close friends, meet someone sympathetic for a coffee or a meal, go for a walk in the country. You are your own best guide to what is right, but remember to keep the balance.

Grieving to time

Neither can you be expected to grieve to order. By that I mean, for example, if you live alone and a relative visits for half an hour twice weekly, you cannot be necessarily expected to grieve at that particular time, just to suit her. Sometimes you can arrange to do that, but do not feel guilty if you cannot.

Work outside the home

Going back to work outside the home can be a hurdle. I suggest going in early and getting the initial shock over, with no audience, or only one or two people. If you don't want to talk about your bereavement, say so. But do not shut people out – they mean well, and most people are awkward and embarrassed with the recently bereaved.

Work in the home

If you have been through a frenzied burst of busy-busy activity, your task will be to slow down and get the balance back. If not, work slowly by stages to your usual level of activity.

Children

I will deal with children and bereavement in Chapter 9. Children need a chance to grieve themselves. They need to see you grieving and not falling apart, to see that it is possible to grieve and then get on with life. This is a good model for their own future lives. But, most important, they need as normal a life as possible.

Support

'Support' is a word bandied about a lot. People seem to mean different things by it. As we tend to regress when grieving, most of us long for the kind of comfort we had, or wish we had, from parents when we were children. We tend to put this expectation onto our friends and relatives, and get disappointed when they are not forthcoming. Often we feel angry, which may be the usual anger at death, but also we tend to blame those not giving us what we are wanting. This is very common. If friends or relatives understand and can take this anger and blame, it can be most therapeutic. However, few are able to do this, and they can get defensive or angry too.

Try spelling out what kind of support you want, and discuss it with your friends and relatives. Ask them if they can give you what you want. Be clear. If they cannot, widen your circle. Spread out the support. You can get different kinds of support from different people – phone calls to check in with you, outings, drives, meals out, loan of books, spiritual help, good conversation, practical help in clearing up the house, shopping and holiday companionship, child minding, and so on.

Difficult moments

For some, getting up in the mornings is the hardest time. If it is for you, you may stay late in bed some days, or even all day occasionally. For others, evenings are the worst, or nights. For many, weekends and Sundays are unbearable.

Try planning ahead. Ask someone to ring you in the morning at a certain time and plan to be up by then. If you haven't one already, maybe you should get a dog; that will get you up and out! Plan your evenings and weekends, even if it's only what TV programmes to watch, or when to weed the garden or mend your socks! Vary your week – a little company, an outing, a treat, some housework or gardening, some TV, reading or whatever. But do not use these to avoid grieving or to suppress feelings. On the other hand, you cannot grieve all of the time.

Sex

If you have lost your sexual partner you will probably begin to miss this side of the relationship after some months. For many people, sex is the only vehicle in their lives for physical contact of a nurturing nature. If this was so for you, it will be even more difficult. But do not try to fill this vacuum by making hasty decisions based on sexual needs, especially with people you don't know well, or who are otherwise attached. You will end up, at best, regretting it and, at worst, in deep trouble.

Try deepening your friendships on an emotional level, which will help somewhat to fill the void. Make new friends too, if you have the inclination. Widen your circle and take up new interests. It will not take away the longing but, at worst, it will distract you a little and, at best, make it bearable.

Disinterest

As time goes on and you begin to recover a little, parts of your life will be returning to normal. You may, to all outward appearances, be coping well and living as you did before your bereavement. But appearances may be deceptive. Life may, and probably has, lost its music for you. I sometimes feel it is as if death has sucked the sap out of life, life has become grey instead of multicoloured. Though acting normally, you are not fully engaged. People with whom you had a good exchange of energy before, leave you flat. Your old interests bore you, new ones fail to excite. The dance is over. The following piece of T. S. Eliot's 'East Coker' from *Four Quartets* gave me insight into this dilemma:

> I said to my soul, be still, and wait without hope
> For hope would be hope for the wrong thing; wait without love
> For love would be love of the wrong thing; there is yet faith
> But the faith and the love and the hope are all in the waiting.
> Wait without thought, for you are not ready for thought:
> So the darkness shall be the light, and the stillness the dancing.
> Whisper of running streams, and winter lightning.
> The wild thyme unseen and the wild strawberry,
> The laughter in the garden, echoed ecstasy
> Not lost, but requiring, pointing to the agony
> Of death and birth.

CHAPTER 6

EMOTIONS, FEELINGS, 'STAGES' OF GRIEF

I explained in the Introduction how we allow realisation of any bad news to sink in slowly, and this is particularly true in the case of death. We do this in order to survive, which is our most basic instinct. Some of the feelings we experience while grieving have been associated together in a particular order and called 'the Stages of Grief'. Elisabeth Kübler-Ross named the most usual stages: denial; anger; bargaining; depression; and acceptance. She also mentioned guilt, fear and hope. Apart from those dealt with so far, there are also many other feelings that can surface at this time, including anxiety, loneliness, abandonment, fatigue, helplessness, powerlessness and despair.

If we are to grieve well and eventually come to terms with our loss, we must not only *feel* the unpleasant feelings, but express them in some way. The most common way is the physical expression of them by crying, sobbing, shouting, shaking and talking. There are, however, other ways that also have a therapeutic result, for example, art work, journalling and some forms of prayer and meditation. Not all these ways are equally effective, however, and they work best combined with the more usual ways of expressing feelings.

Anger

Most of us hate when people are angry with us. Sometimes it makes us feel afraid. We also hate to feel angry ourselves or to express our anger with others. We usually feel guilty about it. Often we turn it in on ourselves as this is less guilt-provoking and easier for those who have a tendency to blame themselves, or to be 'victims' – 'it's always my fault'.

All kinds of things make us angry, including death. This, I believe, is mainly because we feel powerless, that is, we feel we had no say in what happened. It is natural to be angry at injustice, and death can so often appear to be 'unfair'.

The anger we feel when bereaved is usually focused on those nearest and dearest. When this anger is first experienced we rationalise it so quickly that we genuinely believe we are angry with X for Y reasons. It is extremely rare to be aware that we are angry because of the death and bereavement. Even when this is pointed out we will not realise it.

So, if you are feeling angry with those close to you, and you have recently been bereaved, at least be open to the possibility that it is really the death that is making you angry. Of course people irritate us frequently, but is your anger out of proportion?

What can you do?

- If the anger is deep and really interfering with relationships and your life, see a professional such as a counsellor or psychotherapist.
- Tell a friend what is happening and express how angry you are.
- Tell God. Pray about it.
- Do some 'violent' exercise while focusing on the anger, like kicking or hitting a ball. You might even break some old crockery in the back yard! (Don't forget to protect your eyes, and pick up the pieces later!)

If a friend or family member has recently been bereaved and is angry with you or others around her, what can you do? First of all, it is not helpful to point out just then that the anger is due to the death. In my experience they always deny it – it just does not occur to them. The best thing (but not the easiest) you can do is to be tolerant! Allow them to let off steam at you for a while anyway. Do not let it go on too long at any one time, for your sake. Do not 'fight back', just listen.

Sometimes bereaved family members rationalise their anger into blaming someone for the death. Often this is a member of the hospital staff where the person died, or sometimes another family member. In the case of the hospital staff, this occasionally ends in litigation. If you have a suspicion or idea that some negligence or malpractice has taken place, at least wait a while before taking irrevocable steps that may involve you in a lot of distress and expense. Make sure you get the best legal advice before embarking on such an undertaking, which may possibly be an outlet for your (very understandable) anger.

Bargaining

A lot of bargaining takes place in the realm of fantasy, imagery or prayer. Often you bargain with God. It is the expression of the 'If I do X will it be okay?' and the 'If only' feelings. It is a last grasp at the hope that maybe this terrible thing hasn't happened. These feelings show that there isn't yet a total realisation of the reality.

Since much bargaining takes place in private and is rarely shared with others, we tend to feel a little ashamed about it. No need to; most people do it at some time or other. We genuinely believe that 'if only' – for example – 'I could talk to the deceased again for ten minutes, I could accept it'. Bargaining is simply another stepping stone in the sea of pain, and don't we need those stepping stones!

Depression

The word 'depression' is used to cover many feelings and states, from sadness to clinical depression, or even despair (which I will deal with separately). Here I will be dealing with the deep sadness of loss, not what is normally called clinical depression. When you permit yourself to feel sadness, you have fully allowed the realisation of what has happened to sink in. It does not mean you will stay with that realisation at all times from now on. You may still feel the unreality of disbelief and shock or anger at times.

At the acute stage of depression you may still have that pain in your chest or solar plexus that feels physical. You may feel 'desperate' and at times feel you cannot go on living.

If you can cry at this point, it will be the best possible way in the long run of helping you to feel better and integrate what has happened. When we talk of crying, we usually mean crying for a few minutes, or a few tears trickling down your cheeks, a few sniffles, a quick blow of the nose and a 'pull yourself together!' That kind of crying is not really enough to express the depth of sorrow and anguish you are experiencing. Remember how you cried as a child? – threw yourself face down on your bed and sobbed and wailed as if it were the end of the world. That would be very healing if you could do it now. If it does happen and comes almost naturally to you, let it happen. Do not be alarmed. You are not 'breaking down'. You are simply 'sobbing your heart out'.

There is only cause to seek help or advice if you are crying all the time; that is, if it interferes with your usual life, and continues even weeks after the death. If possible, don't do it all alone. Go to a friend's house and cry, or when someone has come to sympathise. Of course we are all alone at times, and grieving is a lonely journey even in the midst of a big family. No one can travel that one for you, anymore than you can journey for the deceased. But again, friends can accompany you on part of the journey.

Clinical depression is usually characterised by one or all of the following: mood swings; sleeplessness, or waking up very early; inability to eat; lack of concentration; loss of memory; and persistent serious thoughts of suicide. If you think you might be clinically depressed, consult your doctor or a psychotherapist.

The type of clinical depression sparked off by a bereavement is called 'reactive depression' and is best treated by psychotherapy or counselling.

Fear

It is quite natural to be afraid of death, other peoples' as well as our own. Fear is a basic survival instinct. I think there are a few very rare, very special people who have worked through and overcome their fear of death. For the vast majority of us ordinary mortals, it is very normal to be afraid. Some of the reasons may be:

- It is facing the unknown.
- It is the end of my existence as I experience it now, i.e. as part of a whole entity, of which my body is a very important part.
- Most humans up to recent times died in pain. Painkillers and anaesthesia are very new and, generally speaking, are only for

the well-off in the northern hemisphere – a small minority of humankind.

So from the moment you hear about an impending death, or that someone you know and love has died, you may feel very fearful. You may feel physical fear resulting in, for example, 'butterflies' in the stomach, dry mouth, 'cotton wool' legs, shaking, shivering, even diarrhoea. Usually these symptoms abate soon, but they may continue, in a mild way, for some considerable time. If they continue to be acute, consult your doctor.

How can you cope with this fear – allay it, live with it?

Unexpressed fears can assume huge proportions, often quite unreal proportions, sometimes simply because they are unexpressed. When you tell someone, and the dark secret fears see the light of day, you will get them into better perspective. So if you can, tell someone, but pick that someone carefully. Try to find a person who does not have the same type of fear. If they do, they may try to comfort you by politely shutting you up, so that their own fear will not be re-stimulated. If you can't think of a suitable 'ear', try a counsellor or therapist, especially if the fear or physical symptoms are interfering with your normal pattern of living, or are persisting acutely over a long period.

There are some other things that you can do that may help allay fears of death:

- Talk to people who are not afraid. Ask them why and how they overcame it. Strange as it may seem, people who have been close to death themselves, or who have had a 'near-death experience', are rarely frightened.
- If you belong to a church or a religion, talk to someone from it. Even if you do not, you can still talk to a religious person or to a member of the clergy.
- Pray or meditate.
- If you are scared about pain, talk to someone who is involved in a pain clinic or hospice. You may be surprised at how well pain can be controlled nowadays, in the developed world at least.
- If your fear is about what may happen to you or the deceased after death, talk to someone from your church or a therapist.

Sometimes this kind of fear comes from early hurts or conditioning.

Your fear may not be of death itself, but of the future stretching out ahead without your loved one. This will slowly fade as you travel on the journey of grief. It is impossible to imagine early on how you will feel in two or three years' time. Could you have imagined two or three years ago how you'd be feeling and coping now?

Another fear is connected with the change in identity brought about by the loss of someone with whom you were closely involved. This too will fade as you work through the grief, as you let the person go emotionally, and as you adjust your identity and invest in someone or something else.

Anxiety

Anxiety can be caused by the same things as fear, but it tends to be less acute. Nevertheless, it can pervade all areas of life. It can interfere with eating, sleep, work, relationships, etc. Friends can get very tired of listening to our anxieties. Anxiety feels the same whether it is justified or imaginary.

If your partner in life has died, and she was the person in the relationship who took responsibility for certain parts of your life, this loss, especially if sudden, can easily provoke anxiety. If this is your situation, it is perfectly normal to feel anxious. Once again, tell someone and ask for help. At first you may be asking for help to carry out some of the tasks your partner took care of. As soon as you can, ask your helper to show you how to perform these tasks yourself.

If you have been left in financial difficulties by your loss, this is a very real problem. Do not be afraid to seek help. Do not be intimidated by bank, social welfare or health board officials. They are there to help and advise. In the case of the last two, they are paid by taxpayers for that purpose. It is your right to consult them. If you are eligible for State subsidy, of one kind or another, that too is your right. You may find it difficult to ask, but don't let those feelings get in the way of what you are due. The embarrassment will only last for a few minutes; the money, hopefully, will help for some time.

Loneliness

The loneliness of travelling this journey of grief on your own is hard to bear, but it is very real and cannot be alleviated totally. No one can travel this for you, they can only be a companion on the way. If you do have companions it can make the journey a lot easier. Most people would be delighted to be asked – wouldn't you? If you have no such companions, professionals such as counsellors can, on occasion, be these companions. They may be limited by professional codes of practice, or overwork, and so unable to give you much more than perhaps a weekly or twice-weekly visit.

Then there is loneliness for the particular person who has died. You can feel this, even when surrounded by family or friends. This loneliness will very gradually fade over the grieving years. However, there will always be a gap that no one else can fill, even a new much-loved partner. Life will never be the same again. It may be equally happy, but never the same.

If the deceased was a constant or even regular companion for certain outings, hobbies, sports, etc., it takes time to adjust to their absence from these roles, and even longer to find a new companion. Others often rally round, but sometimes fail to realise the deep aching gap that you are feeling inside. There are some people you can tell; others just will not understand.

Be kind to yourself. Do what *you* want. If you do not want to go out to a particular place or social occasion because the pain of loneliness is too acute, do not go. Only you know that staying at home alone can be a lot less painful.

Especially in the early days of grieving, many people get comfort from staying around the home they shared with the deceased. Many people say they get a strong feeling of the deceased's presence and find this comforting.

If you feel like that, go with it, listen to your own inner voice. If you feel people would not understand, then don't tell them. But you would be surprised how many people have experienced this.

It is very important to get a balance. I am not suggesting you stay in all the time but for the first weeks. Do what helps you most. This feeling of the deceased's presence in your home will fade. It is a normal stage to go through and you are not hallucinating or going mad. Keep the balance; go out sometimes, do not become a recluse.

Abandonment

Many people have had feelings of being abandoned as children. It doesn't mean anything so dramatic as being left in a basket on a doorstep! Many of us as children spent periods in hospital. Most of us got lost at one time or another. Some of us felt abandoned on our first day at school. Some of us have been fostered, or adopted, or looked after by relatives for a time. And most of us survived these experiences and may even have forgotten them.

When someone close to us dies, these feelings can be re-stimulated and so we may feel abandoned by the deceased. As a result, we can feel more angry, or more afraid, hopeless, powerless, guilty, etc. than we would feel if we had not had those experiences in the past.

If you do experience feelings of abandonment, check the reality of what has happened, and if you have felt like that ever before, especially as a child.

If the death was self-inflicted, this feeling can be very strong. In this case, yes you have been left, but not abandoned. Abandonment is always a child's feeling. It is the feeling of someone left very alone, powerless and helpless in a big dangerous world. No matter how badly you feel now, this is not the case. I will deal further with suicide and with children's reactions to death in other chapters.

Fatigue

Fatigue, or extreme tiredness, can be experienced in many ways by the bereaved – in body, mind, emotions and spirit, frequently in all four. It is a natural reaction to what the whole person experiences as a threatening situation.

Often, we are tired from lack of sleep, and the hard work of a physical, mental and emotional grieving. The 'euphoria' we experience, or 'busyness' to avoid feeling, can be very tiring. If you cannot sleep, rest. Try listening to some relaxing music, or whatever helps you. If you really need sleep, ask your doctor for some mild sleeping medication.

If you are sleeping 'too much', check if it really is too much. Your body may be telling you that you are tired and need sleep to 'knit up the unravelled sleeve of care'. Listen to your own inner voice. Don't push yourself at this time.

Helplessness and powerlessness

As I have said, we are in one sense helpless and powerless in the face of the mystery of death. It is a most unpleasant feeling. Like the feeling of abandonment, some of that terrible hopeless, powerless feeling comes from childhood, when we were, to different degrees, *actually* helpless. This was largely due to our size and lack of physical power and skills, but also to the way most people treat children in our society.

Although it may be that you do not have complete power over death and dying, you can alleviate some of the childhood feelings by taking as much control as possible in the situation. This means taking as much charge as possible of the arrangements, making decisions and participating in the many jobs, gatherings, family meetings, rituals and ceremonies.

You may initially feel unable to do some of this. You may feel too shocked or generally upset. I urge you strongly, though, to push yourself a little, get some support, but take charge.

Of course, if you are not the deceased's partner, the executor of the will, or chief mourner, it may not be possible for you to take charge. If you are a family member or very close friend, you could ask the person who is making the decisions how you could join in or if there is some job you could take on. Even if you are not very close, or seen to be by others, there are usually many jobs to be done, like letting people know what has happened, driving people, collecting them at the airport, from buses or trains, minding children, cooking or bringing ready-to-eat food to the family house.

Despair

I suppose we are all touched by despair at times. I consider despair to be a crisis of meaning, no matter how short-lived. What is life all about? Is this it? Death often brings us up short against these questions. However, they do not always lead us to despair.

This I believe is where the 'turning point' can be found. Early on in grieving you may feel despair at times and at this point I think you should not try to figure it out too much. Confide in someone, seek comfort from friends or a counsellor, express your feelings and find ways to help you get through the pain. But, as time goes by, and moments or longer periods of despair surface, this may be the time to stand back awhile from life. Take a long look at life in general, and yours in particular. Take stock of things. At this time, questions regarding your religion and spirituality come up, questions about your relationships, work, career, and what you want to do with your life, maybe even why you are here on this planet at this time. It feels terrible, but you could look on this crisis time as a gift. Remember, the glass is half full!

It feels much more comfortable to suppress these questions, with alcohol, drugs, food or whatever, keep 'busy-busy', and slowly get back to your old ways of living and coping.

I challenge you to use this gift, this time of opportunity to get off the treadmill for a period, stand back, take stock, stop. Stop and think, read, talk to people who might help – older people, wiser people, young people, spiritual people, people you admire.

Read about personal growth and spirituality, or read about people who have led interesting, exciting or 'meaningful' lives. Read about religion, philosophy, psychology – especially read poetry.

And when you have taken the time out – thought, talked and read – possibly you will go back to the same life as you had previously and do the same things as you did before. But that is not the point. *You* will be different.

Hope

'Hope springs eternal.' If you feel hopeless at times, even close to despair, hope will return. Hope is something I believe to be intrinsic to human nature. People even experience hope in concentration camps. However, hope can be a myriad of different things and, in seemingly hopeless situations, hope seems to narrow down to smaller expectations.

When you are in the throes of sorrow, you may hope for anything from a good night's sleep, to being able to manage on your weekly allowance. When such hope begins to be fulfilled, you may dare to hope for greater things. If it was your partner who died, you may even eventually hope to meet a new partner!

When people grow older they frequently find hope in the next generation. This is one of the reasons they take such great interest and delight in relationships with grandchildren. For people who have not had children or grandchildren, it is more difficult. They often hope for progress where their interests lie in the world.

And there is, of course, hope for the life after death, for peace, happiness, joy, fulfilment and reunion with those we love who have preceded us. Nothing can truly take this hope away from us.

Guilt

One of the main ways we are taught and trained in our culture is by the installation of guilt at an early age. Rabbi Harold S. Kushner, in *When Bad Things Happen to Good People*, has an interesting angle on guilt. He suggests that because we are punished as children when we do something wrong, and this punishment feels 'bad', later, when we feel this same 'bad' feeling for any reason, we make, at a deep level, the same connection learned so young, and feel as if we have done something wrong, i.e. we feel guilty.

Guilt is very often felt as part of grieving – I suggest for the above reason. There is always something to feel guilty about if you search your conscience hard enough!

In every relationship there are difficulties. When someone has died we usually remember these difficulties. At first we often 'idealise' the deceased, praise her out of all proportion and feel she did no wrong. Obviously at this point, any difficulties experienced will feel like *your* fault. How could it be the fault of anyone so wonderful as the deceased? Try to be aware that what you are doing is blaming yourself.

Later, you can sort out what was your fault and what was hers. Often you will realise that the 'blame' was quite evenly distributed.

In some cases, of course, there may be memories of times when you could have done things better, or differently. If that worries or upsets you, talk to someone. It may help to talk to a priest or a spiritual director. Prayer can help.

It can be helpful to imagine yourself apologising to the deceased and imagining what she would say in reply. In my experience of doing this, the deceased almost always understands completely, from their own perspective.

I will deal with guilt after suicide and guilt in bereaved children in later chapters.

Conclusion

It is very likely that you will not have experienced all of these feelings. It depends to a large extent on your past history. All grieving people will experience some of them.

The most important thing to remember is that your feelings, though an important part of you, are just that – a part. You are more than your feelings, even more than a combination of body, mind, feelings and spirit. Think about that. You may find the following useful. It is from a book called *The Unfolding Self: Psychosynthesis & Counselling* by Molly Young Brown, published by the Psychosynthesis Press.

Sit in a comfortable position, relax your body, and allow your breathing to become slow and deep. When you feel ready, read (or have someone read to you) the following:

> I have a body, but I am not my body. My body may itself be in different conditions of health or sickness, it may be rested or tired, but that has nothing to do with myself, my real 'I'. I value my body as my precious instrument of experience and action in the world, but it is only an instrument. I treat it well. I seek to keep it in good health, but it is not myself. I have a body, but I am not my body *(pause)*.

> I have emotions, but I am not my emotions. My emotions are many different feelings, always changing, sometimes confusing. They may swing from love to hatred, from calm to anger, from joy to sorrow, and yet my essence, my true nature, does not change. I remain. Though I may be temporarily washed by a wave of emotion, I know it will pass in time; therefore, I am not this emotion. Since I can observe and understand my emotions,

and learn to direct, utilise and integrate them harmoniously, it is clear that they are not myself. I have emotions, but I am not my emotions *(pause)*.

I have a mind, but I am not my mind. My mind is a valuable tool of discovery and expression, but it is not the essence of my being *(pause)*.

My thoughts are constantly changing with new ideas, knowledge and experience. Often my mind refuses to obey me! Therefore it cannot be me, myself. It is an organ of knowledge of both the inner and the outer worlds, but it is not myself. I have a mind, but I am not my mind *(pause)*.

Next comes the stage of identification with one's self. As you read, open yourself to the experience the words evoke:

If I am not body, feelings, or mind, what am I? I recognise and affirm that I am a centre of pure self-awareness. I am a centre of will, capable of observing, directing, and using all my psychological processes and my physical body. I am the one who is aware. I am the one who chooses.

PART III

SPECIFIC KINDS OF GRIEF AND GRIEVING

CHAPTER 7

GRIEVING PARTICULAR DEATHS

As I have said, how we react to death and bereavement depends more on our individuality and personal history than on the cause of death or the manner in which it occurred. However, there are some issues connected with particular deaths or ways of dying that are different and that present specific difficulties. There are some feelings that are more likely to be evoked in different circumstances. In this chapter, I want to address briefly these specific difficulties and give some guidelines that may prove useful.

Invisible Mourners

Mourning is a public as well as private affair. As social animals, the acknowledgement of our loss by society forms an important part in the grieving process, particularly in working through feelings of numbness, denial and isolation.

The mourners play a central role in the institutional and social rituals that our society has created for grieving. The role of the family and extended family is still pivotal to society's acknowledgement of the loss. However, there are some circumstances in which, for various reasons, mourners are unable to receive this public acknowledgement of their loss. They are deprived, therefore, of a large part of the grieving process. There is, as it were, a gap in the process, which is difficult to fill in any other way.

In most cases, when someone dies, there are people who knew them in particular situations or circumstances not known to the close relatives or family. They may have shared some specific or special experiences or moments with the deceased, or have seen or known a particular side of her character. Often those friends or acquaintances are not close to the deceased at the time of death. Perhaps the special moments they shared were not prolonged or of great importance to anyone else. These people are also bereaved, they too have suffered a loss and need to grieve.

Intensity of feeling at the time of a death is influenced by the type of relationship with the deceased, but more by what the bereaved person had invested in the relationship. It can easily be understood, therefore, that many people can experience intense feelings of loss when someone, not necessarily perceived by society to be close to them, dies. Sometimes the deceased may not have been aware of the degree of intensity. People have even been known to grieve when fictitious characters in radio or TV soaps die. Death, as I have explained previously, triggers memories of other deaths and losses in a different way for each individual. For various reasons, the people grieving in the following ways can be in the position of an 'invisible mourner':

- Those grieving unborn babies lost through miscarriage, abortion or stillbirth.
- Those grieving very young children.
- Those grieving pets.
- Those grieving a homosexual partner or lover.
- Those grieving a divorced or separated partner.
- Those grieving, who have been involved with the deceased in any form of secret or covert relationship for whatever reason.

If you find yourself in this situation, you are going to need a great deal of support. Your aim must be to grieve as well as you can in the circumstances, and to be as open or public as possible, always considering your own feelings and those of all the people involved.

In situations where you were involved in a 'secret' relationship, for whatever reason, there is often a temptation at the time of your friend or lover's death, to blurt it out, 'come out', or confront those who knew nothing about your connection with the deceased. Think first. The pain of grief may be driving you. You may feel that such actions will bring relief. They may not, or if they do, the relief may be very temporary. You may make things a lot more difficult for yourself and also for others. As a general rule, wait a while, do your grief work, and leave decisions like these for at least six months to a year.

The degree of invisibility of a mourner varies according to the reason of the invisibility and the feelings of the mourner. In the case of grieving a pet, the main reason for invisibility may be fear of ridicule; in the case of a homosexual partner, fear of being subjected to homophobia and gay oppression or of betraying a trust or upsetting the family if the relationship was very secret.

The reason for the invisibility influences what you can do if you find yourself in the situation of an invisible mourner. But whatever the reason, you are going to need a great deal of support. Confide in someone, preferably a friend. If you cannot tell a friend, go to a counsellor or therapist, or ring a counselling helpline or the Samaritans. Once you have told even one person, you are no longer completely 'invisible'.

If you have been unable to attend or participate in the usual funeral rituals, you may wish to create your own. See Chapter 12.

Whatever the reason that your grieving has to be 'invisible', never forget that it is no less legitimate, and that your grief and pain are no less real. Your grieving process will be similar to that of others who can be more open and public about it. Be kind and compassionate to yourself, and make allowances for yourself at this time.

Death of Pets

The effect of the death of a pet on children is addressed in Chapter 9. For an adult, the death of a pet can also be a painful loss. For many adults, particularly the elderly and those living alone, their pet is their close companion and sometimes their best friend. While grieving a pet, you can also be in the position of the 'invisible mourner', as many people would not acknowledge or understand your loss as warranting 'real' grief.

Most of what I have written in this book about what helps when experiencing loss through a death, also applies when grieving for a beloved animal. The problem is that society in general does not acknowledge that.

If your pet was your close friend and companion, then that is what you are grieving – a close friend and companion, regardless of what anybody else says or thinks.

All the involvement in the dying and death of your pet helps the grieving, just as it does when a human loved one dies. When humans die, there is, in most cases, a generally accepted ritual for the funeral and disposal of the remains. However, in the case of animals, you have a lot more power to make decisions and influence what happens. You are permitted in law even to make a decision for euthanasia in the case of animal friends, and to bury them in your own garden if you wish. If your pet is diagnosed as terminally ill, or is seriously injured in an accident, you can decide to nurse it at home. In some cases the vet will keep it in the surgery for various treatments, or you may be given the choice of having your pet's life terminated. This choice is never an easy one, and should not be taken lightly or too hurriedly.

If your pet is a valued friend and companion, the decision for euthanasia is a painful one. Many people do not understand that, and have the attitude that your pet is 'only an animal'. This attitude can result in your feeling, at worst, silly and sentimental, at best, misunderstood.

Nowadays, vets are usually sympathetic to your feelings. If you are in doubt as to such a decision, discuss it with her. Do not be embarrassed to disclose how important your pet is to you.

If you do decide to allow the vet to end your pet's life, she may ask you if you would like to hold the animal while the lethal injection is administered. You may, understandably, feel fearful about this. Ask the vet any questions you wish. If you feel you cannot hold your pet, you can ask the vet if someone else – her nurse, assistant, colleague – will hold your pet. If you do decide to hold it, don't be ashamed to cry, but try to remain calm until the animal has died, as they can sense your feelings.

If you have facilities, you may wish to bury your pet in your own garden or on your land. This allows you time to say goodbye to your friend and have a ritual or funeral. If you do this, you can be creative as to how you organise it all. This involvement in decision-making and in creating whatever kind of send-off you want for your pet is extremely therapeutic, and will contribute to the quality of your grieving and healing the loss, just as it does with the loss of a human loved one.

Afterwards, be open about your loss, and share your feelings with friends. People bereaved through the death of a pet often come to professional counsellors or psychotherapists who are quite used to it, so there is no need to feel embarrassed or ashamed of those feelings.

Death of a pet, as with any death, reminds you of other deaths and losses, and can be a time to do some unfinished grieving for another death or loss.

Friends may encourage you to get another pet immediately after yours has died. I suggest you wait until you have done some grieving for the last one before making a new relationship and commitment – which it is, regardless of how others perceive it.

Missing Persons

A particularly agonising form of bereavement is the loss of a loved one who is 'missing', when you do not even know if indeed they have died.

The uncertainty of not knowing tends to block people at the stage of denial. This happens even when the evidence of death is quite conclusive, or the time has been so long that death seems to be the inevitable conclusion.

And yet, you can never be sure. You hear stories of people who have turned up after X number of years, you feel a surge of hope, and you hang onto that hope for 'dear life'.

Can you grieve, can you let go and move on, get on with your life?

Yes, you can. Of course it is not easy, but you can. In addressing this, I am referring to the loss of persons who have either been missing for a very long time, or whom police and other responsible bodies believe to be dead.

At this stage you must work towards letting them go, as if they have died. It does not necessarily mean that you believe they have died. But they have been lost to you, whether still alive or not. You are bereaved, whether they are dead or not. And if by any chance they are found, or return, you will be dealing with a different person in so many ways, and you are different too after all you have gone through. The old relationship has gone, has died.

And so, you need to start grieving very much as you would if they were dead. Allow yourself to feel the grief and loss, to be angry and guilty, hopeless and sad. Cry if you can, talk about your loved one, reminisce.

Have a ritual or rituals and involve others in creating and participating in them. It will be different from a ritual marking a death; it will be a ritual marking a loss. Acknowledge the real situation in the ritual. Build into it a part for loss and possible death, a part for uncertainty and a part for hope.

If your loved one is missing because of work, or involvement in a movement or organisation you support and believe in, such as a soldier lost during a war, your pride in them and perhaps shared ideals may help to console you. Perhaps she was doing what she wanted to do, or believed in, and if she died, she died in what she, and maybe you, believe to be a just cause, or so that others may live. That can be a great comfort.

Bereaved People with a Mental Handicap

This is a group in our society who are often treated as invisible when bereaved. For some reason, it is often believed that they do not have similar reactions and feelings to the rest of us when they are bereaved. Their grief is often not acknowledged.

If you have been bereaved recently, and have a mental handicap, or know someone in this situation, remember we all grieve differently. Every person's grief must be acknowledged and their way of grieving respected.

People with a mental handicap often have little power over their lives, and therefore the powerlessness grief evokes can feel even stronger. This is very frightening, and it is important to acknowledge that fear, and provide for how it may affect them.

Be straight with them. They are still the same person you know and love and communicate with when they are bereaved. They do not change any more as a result of it than anyone else when they experience a loss. They may need more time for you to explain what has happened in their language. Take time, and answer all their questions simply but, above all, honestly.

Because we often fail to acknowledge their grief, we often exclude people with mental handicap from what is happening in a family when someone is dying, or has died, and from the funeral and other rituals and services.

Ask them how they would like to be included, but presume they *will* be included unless they specifically decide to exclude themselves. Encourage them to join with you, to be part of all that is happening, part of the family. They may be fearful and need a lot of reassurance. Take the time to give it.

Death After a Long Illness

When someone has been seriously ill over a long period, you do get some opportunity to do what is called 'anticipatory grieving'. It is believed that this helps in the eventual grieving process. It does help to lessen the feelings of shock, denial and disbelief in the early stages, but it does not eliminate them.

If the deceased has suffered greatly, either mentally or physically, you may feel glad when they eventually die. This sense of relief is for the end of their *suffering*, of course, not because they have *died*. It often cushions the pain of losing them in the early days. It may fade as time goes on, and cease to make the loss any less painful. In fact, what often replaces it are graphic nightmarish memories of the person suffering. These pictures may be difficult to banish, especially at the times when you are most sensitive, like when you are going to sleep or first wake up in the morning. These will fade eventually, but can cause you a lot of distress. It helps to describe them in detail, and maybe over and over again, to someone who was not close to the deceased. Professional counsellors or psychotherapists are useful in this respect.

If you have been involved in the care of the deceased during her last illness, you may be exhausted after her death. Take a long rest. This does not necessarily mean opting out of life, which may make some people depressed, but taking time doing whatever is restful for you. You will also now have a big gap in your life, not only an emotional gap as is usual with all bereavement, but a physical gap. Nursing a terminally ill person, especially if you are close to them, is physically exhausting and emotionally draining. It is also time-consuming. After their death, there is so much time. You may not feel that at first, as you will be recovering your strength, and probably tidying up and perhaps settling all their affairs.

However, as time goes on and your energy returns, you may find that the purpose of your life has been removed. In fact, it has. Acknowledge this, and realise it is bound to affect you. Do not jump straight into some other activity, especially caring for another seriously ill person. Stand back and consider what you truly want to do with your life. Try not to make any major decisions for at least a year.

As time goes on, you will remember the whole of your loved one's life, the good times and the bad, and not only the distress of her last illness.

Death from AIDS

Much of what I have said about death after a long-drawn-out illness also applies to death from AIDS. I do not intend to focus on the physical symptoms and effects of AIDS, but on some of the specific difficulties in grieving for someone who has died of this cruel disease.

Although the climate is improving, albeit extremely slowly, there is still a considerable stigma attached to contracting the AIDS/HIV virus. This is not the place to comment or make moral judgements. However, this stigma does affect the grieving of those left behind. Not only have they to suffer the pain of the loss, but the anguish of knowing that some people are probably passing judgement on the lifestyle or behaviour of someone they have loved and lost.

If you find yourself in this position, focus on what you knew, loved and remember about your loved one. Focus on the one you knew, not on what others say in judgement.

If you and your family and friends wish to keep it a secret that the deceased died of AIDS, that is your privilege, it is your right to make such a decision. Do not let anyone force you to be more open than you feel able to be.

However, secrets tend to compound embarrassment and shame, and may, instead of helping, cause you to feel more ashamed of yourself and your loved one. If you are able, without adding too much to your stress and pain, be open, talk about her, be proud.

Meeting with others bereaved through AIDS can be helpful, even if, at first, you do not feel comfortable. Maybe you feel you have little in common with them, other than the obvious. Persevere. This tragedy that you have in common is a strong binding force, a link that could bring you a great deal of comfort.

If your loved one was part of a community or a group living a particular lifestyle, meeting and mixing with the group can help to lift the shame and embarrassment.

Being open and explicit about death from AIDS can also help to educate and to change public opinion, and thus reduce the stigma and associated shame and embarrassment for others in your position. But do what is right for you, in your particular situation.

Death by Suicide

Society's attitude to suicide is key in how you grieve after someone has taken their own life. There is still considerable stigma attached to suicide. This stigma not only causes and increases shame and guilt, but makes it even more difficult for the bereaved to find support from family and friends. For this reason, professional help from a counsellor or psychotherapist is often useful.

Guilt, in other circumstances, is a useful aid to our distinguishing right actions from wrong. It is a normal result of a healthily functioning conscience. Normally it is a helpful guide, and does not linger once you have made a decision to right or make amends for the wrongdoing.

In the case of social stigma, there may be wrongdoing involved or there may not. Whichever it is, and whether we know which it is, the action taken often engenders a degree of guilt or shame out of proportion or quite inappropriate to the act, and spreading far beyond the perpetrator to family, extended family and friends. Such it is with suicide. To deal with guilt and shame:

- Acknowledge it.
- Sort out if you have done anything to be guilty or feel shame about. This is difficult, and usually requires outside or professional help.
- If you have, try to understand and forgive yourself, or ask understanding and forgiveness from others.
- If you have not, talk it out, with help. Express the feelings and then let it go.
- Think about the deceased – the kind of person she was, and your relationship with her. Make up your own mind. Hold on to that decision if others criticise or make thoughtless or cruel remarks.

Anger is one of the other feelings closely associated with suicide. With any death, we can feel angry with the deceased, but with suicide it is often very strong, even overwhelming for a time.

To deal with your anger:

- Acknowledge it and acknowledge to what it belongs.
- Try not to vent it on those close to you who are not responsible for the death.
- If you have a friend, counsellor or therapist, spend some time expressing your anger with them.
- Write a letter to the deceased, expressing your anger. You may like to burn it, or 'offer it up' in some kind of ritual.
- Forgive the deceased, but do not try to do this until you have taken the previous steps.
- Forgive yourself.

Death by Murder, Terrorism, or in War Situations

Death in any of these violent ways is often a public affair, and some of the grieving may have to be done in public. You may be involved in a lot of bureaucracy, such as questioning by the police, a post-mortem, public enquiries, investigations, inquests and court trials. You may be interviewed, photographed or filmed by the media when you are most shocked, angry or in your deepest grief. This is often something you have no control over. These particular kinds of deaths often evoke that powerless feeling I have mentioned in Chapter 6 and exacerbate it. For that reason, try, amidst your grief, to be clear and definite about whom you wish to talk to, where and when. You will need to tell all those around you, so that you can be supported in doing what you really want. If you have to speak or appear in public, or on the media, try to rehearse with a friend beforehand what you wish to do or say.

With many of these deaths, the investigations and repercussions can go on and on, sometimes for years. You will find it extremely difficult to move through the grief and eventually to let go of the deceased, when there are so many reminders, often quite traumatic, even requiring you to 're-live' the whole event.

If this is happening to you, acknowledge the problem and make allowances for it in your grieving and letting-go process. You may benefit from the help of a counsellor or psychotherapist, particularly when:

- You sense you may be ready to move on, but you cannot rid yourself of reminders 'hanging over' you.
- You are experiencing 'flashbacks', or distressingly vivid memories are intruding into your consciousness inappropriately.
- You have to be involved in a case, inquest, enquiry or commemoration.

If the deceased was involved in an army or organisation they felt strongly about, you may glean some comfort from knowing they were killed in a cause they believed in and in which they were engaged in furthering.

On occasions, you may be fearful of reprisals or revenge threatening your family or others in your organisation or community. This fear may interfere with your grieving. Once you have attended to the situation on a practical level, enlist the help of a counsellor or psychotherapist.

You may find yourself obsessed with who killed your loved one, or who was responsible for the death. Whether you know or not, you may be preoccupied or obsessed with revenge and retribution.

This anger is quite usual but needs an outlet. You should find someone, preferably a counsellor or psychotherapist, to help you to express these feelings in a safe place, where you cannot hurt yourself – or anyone else. They will also help you to figure out what practical steps you can and cannot take to see that justice is done.

You may feel that having the perpetrator punished will heal your grief, or close the door on the whole episode. It is seldom like that. Outward events and actions do help tremendously, but you must also do your own private inner grief work.

In many situations, such as war or bombing, you may never see the deceased's body, as it may have been lost, buried abroad, or mutilated beyond recognition. This adds considerably to the usual feelings of denial and disbelief, as well as anger and powerlessness. Seek professional help and be sure to involve yourself in some ritual, even if you have to create your own, privately.

When your loved one has been, or you perceive them to have been, killed deliberately, there may be public or other pressure on you to 'forgive' the perpetrator. This is a tremendous thing to do, in time. Do not try to forgive before you have grieved and expressed your anger, in a safe situation of course. (See Chapter 6.)

You may never feel you have forgiven. That is quite normal. Maybe all you can do is not act out your angry or vengeful feelings. That may be sufficient. What might help is to remember that bottled-up anger and revenge hurt you more than anyone else. Contrary to the old adage, to forgive is human, but only after time and a great deal of hard work on your part.

Accidental Death

The effects of accidental death on the bereaved vary, of course, depending not only on the bereaved person, but on the type of accident and whether or not the bereaved person was involved in the accident.

If you have survived an accident in which others were killed, you have suffered a double trauma and you must take that into consideration in your grieving.

The stage of denial, numbness and shock can persist for a much longer period than is usual with other types of death. You may remember that we naturally let go of the pain of loss gradually, as a defence mechanism, and so it is important to respect it for the protection it is providing for you. Be gentle with yourself.

If you are not believing, or not feeling, the loss of your loved one, do not worry. Concentrate on your own healing, physical if necessary, as well as the mental and emotional shock of the trauma. This denial of reality may be exacerbated if you were unable to attend the funeral due to your own injuries. In that case, try to organise some kind of ritual of passing when you are well enough. If both your own trauma and the loss of the deceased are hitting you together, try to take it slowly, step by step, 'one day at a time'. It will take you much longer to complete your grieving: acknowledge this and be patient. This is another situation where professional help may be useful.

Accidental death is usually sudden and violent, and so feelings arising from these aspects should also be considered. If you were not involved in the accident yourself, besides the suddenness and violence, you may be involved in identifying your loved one. If so, bring along someone close and sympathetic, but who is not too involved with the deceased. They can then be present for you and not too overcome by their own feelings. Do not be afraid or ashamed to cry or show feelings. Give yourself time just afterwards to talk about the whole experience.

If the body of the deceased has not been recovered, or is damaged beyond recognition, try to involve as much ritual as if the remains were present. Ritual is an essential part of the grief process. (See Chapter 12.)

With accidents come feelings of 'if only', and thoughts and fantasies of what 'might have been'. Often with these you will be blaming yourself. You may blame yourself for surviving when your loved one has died. These are quite usual, 'normal' feelings. If they persist over a long period, or are associated with shame and guilt, seek professional help, or that of a good friend who will listen to you and help you to tease it out, and not reassure you too quickly.

Your Fault

Sometimes, tragically, for any number of reasons, someone may be responsible for another's death. I am not referring here to guilt feelings that arise in most grieving, but to circumstances when you have killed, or are directly responsible for the death of another person. In this case you will certainly need and should seek help in many forms, but particularly professional counselling or psychotherapy.

Whether the death was accidental or you deliberately killed someone, or you are not sure which, whether you knew or were close to the deceased or not – all of this will affect how you react, including how long it will take you to recover. You certainly will never forget it, but, like all traumas, it will fade with help, work and time.

Remember, if you knew or were close to the deceased, you are also bereaved and need to grieve. To do this, you must find someone to be with you in your grief who will not judge you, or at least understand your need to grieve.

You may feel a need to be punished. If that is to happen, others will look after it – do not punish yourself. Guilt and shame may overwhelm you. Get some help, from a professional counsellor, psychotherapist, priest, religious person or spiritual guide, and try to follow the steps I mentioned regarding guilt and shame in the section on suicide earlier in this chapter.

As far as possible, be with people who are not too angry with you and can maintain a non-judgemental attitude. It is not necessary to love the action or behaviour in order to love or understand the person responsible for it.

CHAPTER EIGHT

GRIEVING FOR CHILDREN

Your children are not your children.
They are the sons and daughters of Life's longing for itself.
They come through you but not from you,
And though they are with you yet they belong not to you.

You are the bows from which your children as living arrows are sent
forth.
The Archer sees the mark upon the path of the infinite, and he
bends you with His might that His arrows may go swift and far.
Let your bending in the Archer's hand be for gladness,
For even as he loves the arrow that flies, so he loves also the bow that
is stable. *(Kahlil Gibran)*

The Death of a Child

Each death has its own anguish for those left behind. Many people would
feel that the death of a child or foetus is particularly poignant. In this
chapter I will try to pinpoint some of the particular difficulties in grieving
the death of children.

I will use the word 'children' to include foetuses, without intending to
imply any particular opinion on the question of when a foetus becomes a
child. My intention is to inform and be of help to those grieving the loss
of a foetus or child at whatever stage of development and whether planned
or unplanned. I will deal with miscarriage, abortion, stillbirth and
neonatal death, cot deaths or SIDS (Sudden Infant Death Syndrome) and,
to a lesser extent, death of children of different ages. This subject deserves
a whole book, so this chapter is not intended to be comprehensive. It
should be helpful not only to parents and step-parents, but also
grandparents, aunts, uncles, godparents, siblings and other relatives and
friends.

The most obvious thing that grieving all these different kinds of death has in common is that a large part of the loss is the loss of something that we have not yet experienced. When anyone dies, to the degree that we were attached to them, we feel as if a part of us has died. When a child dies, the loss of our hopes and dreams, which were also a part of us, is a very real loss in itself. This applies to all grieving, but it is felt more acutely when a child dies. It is the loss of the fulfilment of potential, of dreams and hopes, of the idea or concept of a specific map of the future.

It may seem strange or paradoxical, but it is extremely difficult to grieve something that we never actually had, in any concrete or normally accepted sense. The kind of dreams, hopes and plans we have for our children are frequently held near to our hearts, and often never shared with anyone, or at most within a very close circle of family or friends. The most helpful thing is to make these hopes and dreams and plans explicit, even if it is only to yourself. In this way you have hopes, dreams and plans that are more real, to grieve and let go of. If you do not wish to share these with anyone, even your partner, close friend, brother or sister, I suggest you write them down. There is some strange way in which pre-verbal (i.e. non-verbalised) thoughts or ideas assume a different and more intense reality when we put them into words.

Whether writing or sharing, let your imagination run. Dare to express all the wildest dreams and hopes and plans you had for that child. This is a very painful process, but a necessary part of grieving the child. Be kind to yourself in this process. If on your own, do only a little at a time. If possible though, share it with someone. If there is not someone close that you trust, maybe you should share it with a counsellor or therapist.

Grieving a Foetus or Unborn Child

The aforementioned difficulty applies, maybe even to a larger extent, to the death of a foetus or unborn child. Added to this is that, when attempting to verbalise your hopes, dreams and plans, you may find it even more difficult, because a) you had been even less explicit to yourself about them, as they were only just beginning to take shape, and b) those around you may be less sympathetic to listening to you in this particular part of the grieving process.

The single most difficult thing about grieving a foetus or unborn child is usually that it is such a private grief. In some cases, it may be the loss of a child through an induced abortion. In that case, it may be a closely guarded secret, for either legal reasons or those of guilt or shame. These latter, of course, do not apply to everyone grieving loss through abortion. I will deal with this later.

Isolation is the predominant feeling for many. This unborn child had not yet become a *separate* member of the society we are part of. Therefore the grieving cannot be the same kind of social event as it is in the case of someone, even a very young child, who has been part of society as a separate identity, for no matter how short a time. The death is often unacknowledged.

I will try below to point out some of the specific difficulties experienced in the death of unborn or stillborn children, and some suggestions as to what might be helpful. These are in no way intended to be comprehensive as, once again, each individual grieves in her own way.

Miscarriage

Besides the difficulties mentioned above, which apply to the death of all unborn children, miscarriage has its own particular problem when grieving.

If the miscarriage is very early on, even you who have experienced it may have difficulty in fully acknowledging that the child existed at all, or died, while you are still left with a feeling of loss.

The attitude of those around you may also be that it never existed, or that if it did, it is quite expendable and replaceable. 'Never mind, you'll have another one soon' or some similar cliché. You can be tempted, in order to comfort yourself, to adopt this so-called 'positive' attitude yourself. This is really denying what has happened, which is that part of you (or of someone) or a separate life, whichever way you look at it, has died. And again you may be left with a feeling of loss, or of something missing.

Miscarriage, especially if you have had more than one, is often accompanied by a feeling of failure in the woman who has experienced it.

Fathers are often shut out or excluded from the whole event. You fathers may feel also that you have to be 'strong' for your partner. For these reasons you often feel that you do not have permission to grieve.

Very often you do not know what has happened to the dead child or you may know it was not buried if it happened a number of years ago.

Even if not 'comforted' with thoughtless clichés, or unlooked-for advice to reproduce an almost instant replacement, you will probably not receive much sympathy. One woman I know, in a country place, alone all day, had not *one* visitor coming to sympathise after losing her second baby.

What can be helpful?

- Do everything you can to help you realise this child really existed. Giving it a name is probably the first and most helpful thing to do, and refer to it afterwards always with that name.

- If you don't know the sex, use two names, or a unisex name. Talk about her existence, and death, to as many people as you feel able.

- Mark the anniversary of the miscarriage each year, or the anniversary of the day the baby was due to be born. Have a ritual or simple ceremony that day each year. If it was your child, try to find out the medical reason for the death. This helps to contradict feelings of guilt or failure.

- Do not have another baby as quickly as possible to 'replace' the one who died. Even tiny babies are individuals, and you cannot 'replace' one with another like a new pair of shoes, until you have grieved the last one.

- Fathers, do not be embarrassed or ashamed to cry or grieve in your own way, or if you are, do it anyway! Crying together with your partner can be healing, and can enrich your relationship.

- Partners, try not to blame each other. Try not to depend solely on each other for support. Take someone outside the close family into your confidence, and lean a little on them.

- Encourage the brothers and sisters of the dead child (if any) to be part of it all too, and to grieve.

- If you had the miscarriage in hospital and don't know what happened to the remains, ask. What you imagine is often worse than the reality. But whatever the reality is, it is easier to grieve if you know the truth. Nowadays all remains are buried. You may arrange a private burial if you wish.

- If you need a friendly neighbour to sympathise, or to come in for a cup of coffee when you're on your own, ask her. She'll be flattered – wouldn't you?

The more you are able to share your loss, and your grieving, the easier it will be to let go and accept what has happened. Also, the easier the climate in society will be for others who have experienced miscarriage.

Stillbirth

Many of the difficulties arising with a stillborn child are similar to miscarriage, but the following are some that are, I think, specific to stillbirth.

- In many cases the mother knows ahead of time that the baby she is carrying is dead. This is not only a time of great anguish, but also a time when the parents are caught in a kind of suspended grief. They know the baby has died, and so 'should' be able to grieve but a) they have no remains, and b) they know they will have to grieve again when the baby is born. They cannot therefore move through the grief. It is a very 'stuck' state.

- In the case of stillbirth, until recently, parents or even the mother rarely saw the baby. The whole thing was regarded as a kind of 'non-event'. Fortunately this is changing, and fast.

- At the 'stage' of anger, it will often be directed against the doctor or medical professionals. The death may or may not have been due to their negligence. Try to get clear of your angry feelings before you take it any further, for example, to the medical council or to court.

- Stillborn babies were sometimes buried in a mass grave with no individual marking, with little ritual, giving the parents no place to focus their grief, and emphasising the 'non-event' it was regarded to be.

- The mother may have been treated with less than total tact and respect in the hospital. Fortunately, this is changing.
- Christian parents, or indeed others, may have worries about whether or not the child was baptised.
- There may have to be a post-mortem, which may be distressing you.

What can help?

- Get in touch with the local stillbirth association if there is one in your area.
- Do some grieving while carrying the dead child. You will have to grieve again when she is born, but this will be a different kind of grieving.
- Make sure to see the baby, if you are a parent or sibling especially. Spend time with her and bring and include other members of the family if you wish. Hold her, talk to her and let others do so also, if they wish. Some people like to take a photograph and gather other mementoes such as a lock of hair.
- Get as much information as possible about why the baby died. This helps to alleviate any guilt.
- Take an opportunity to express any anger with a counsellor or trusted friend, before taking any legal action.
- Have a funeral or ritual, and attend the burial if possible. Burial in a family grave with grandparents or other family members is often comforting for parents.
- If you, as a mother, were not respected, or treated well and tactfully in the hospital, address it with them, not in your anger, but assertively. This will help you to overcome feelings of being a victim of helplessness or powerlessness, and may help others who find themselves in the same situation.
- If you are worried about baptism, consult a priest or minister from your own denomination, preferably a hospital chaplain.

Cot death or Sudden Infant Death Syndrome (SIDS)

Once again, some of the difficulties are common to the death of all babies, but there are some that are specific.

- The fact is that there is no definite known cause of cot death, and so no matter how hard you try, you may never find out definitely the cause of death.
- The involvement of the police and legal formalities, including post-mortem and inquest, can add to the difficulties.
- You may worry that it may affect your other living children or any you may have in the future. This then affects decision-making regarding having further children.

What can help?

- Get in touch with your local sudden infant death association.
- Find out all research and information regarding SIDS so that you can be as fully informed as possible (though there is still no definite known cause). The association can help with this.
- Involve all the family and extended family. Mothers, do not exclude fathers or other children or grandparents, if they wish to be involved.
- Get support. Have a friend or members of the association with you when dealing with police, etc. You may wish to consult a solicitor.
- Keep the memory of the dead child alive in the ways suggested previously.

Death of Older Children

As I have said, the death of any child is particularly poignant. There is such a strong sense of unfulfilment. A child is so often the 'life and soul of the house'. The sound of silence will be so much the louder.

This applies to all children, from toddlers to teenagers. There are, of course, a myriad of specific ways in which the particular children are missed, yearned for, and grieved. As different children carry different roles in a family, so the family is affected differently, for example, when the 'clown' or the 'peacemaker' or the 'wild one' has gone.

Children's friends, who it must be remembered are also grieving, may continue to visit the house for months or even years to come. Sometimes they could be encouraged to play or 'rap' in the dead child's bedroom or den. Some families encourage this and it gives them (the parents) great comfort. More of this in Chapter 12 on ritual.

Whatever the age of the child that died, from weeks in the womb to young adults, they can never be replaced. No one should even try. Every individual is unique and irreplaceable and deserves to be fully mourned and grieved, as completely and with as much respect, reverence and ritual as any adult.

> It is not growing like a tree
> In bulk, doth make Man better be;
> Or standing long an oak, three hundred year,
> To fall a log at last, dry, bald, and sere:
> A lily of a day
> Is fairer far in May
> Although it fall and die that night –
> It was the plant and flower of Light.
> In small proportions we just beauties see;
> And in short measures life may perfect be. *(Ben Jonson)*

Grieving Other Relationships

There are also specific difficulties attached to death and grieving for other relationships, for example, death of parents, siblings, grandparents, lovers, spouses, partners of various kinds, close friends and even pets. Many books have been written about all of these bereavements. Suffice here to say that I believe that most of the differences and difficulties experienced by the bereaved person are determined by her physical make-up, upbringing, and past hurts of all kinds, especially all experiences of loss and death, and how she coped with them. The differences will not be determined by the relationship to the deceased, but will be dependent on the degree of attachment in the relationship. Also, differences are largely dependent on the type of attachment there was to the deceased.

CHAPTER 9

BEREAVED CHILDREN

Children's reaction to death, and how they deal with loss and bereavement, deserves a whole book to itself. This chapter is intended simply to give you a chance to look at the most useful attitude to adopt with bereaved children, and to give some guidelines on how best to help them cope. I will use some examples, which hopefully will stimulate your creativity as an adult dealing with a bereaved young person. These examples are not models in themselves to be copied or used as any kind of formula. As Alan Watts said, 'Don't confuse the signpost with the destination!'

General Attitude

How to explain the mystery of death to a child? We often use as an excuse that they are too young to understand (whatever their age!). As a result of this attitude, we either allow them to be around and involved in dying and death without any discussion or explanation, or we deliberately hide from them all evidence that death has occurred, sometimes even omitting to tell them! This behaviour is simply a reflection of a misguided attitude to the whole subject.

Of course children can understand death, but to different degrees, depending on age, intelligence and past experiences of many kinds.

Children's age and bereavement

Opinions vary as to how children of different ages are affected by loss, death and bereavement. I don't find that making distinctions about how to treat children according to their age is very useful. Just as with adults, young people should be treated as individuals. Most parents or guardians will have a good sense of how the death has affected the child. Every child, no matter the age, is affected by the death of someone close to them, or close to their parents or carers.

The skill is to gauge at what *level* the child can understand, and most of that comes from listening to the child herself. The child will ask, if the climate is right. Listening well to the question is the clue to giving the right answer. (Of course, there is no 'right' answer, only an appropriate one!).

The right climate is dependent largely on the attitude and state of adults and other children around. If adults are fearful, the child will pick up the fear.

Early conditioning

Until recently, death was very much a part of life for all the community. Children, even toddlers, trotted in and out of wakes when dead people were laid out. They were brought to funerals and burials and little was hidden from them. They learned so early that death is part of everyday living, that they never knew any other way of looking at it. This does not mean they were not upset in all the ways adults are – shocked, angry, sad, guilty, fearful, etc. But they were able to cope with and express these feelings more easily, and adjust better to life again, after a time.

Because a lot of these customs, which involved children, are fading out, it does not mean that you have to abandon them. You can bring up your child whatever way you want. No one will physically restrain you from involving your child in death, dying, wakes, funerals, burials and grieving. They may try to advise you against it, even preach intellectual superiority.

Tiny children, babies, are affected mostly through the effect the death has had on those close to them, especially the mother or main carer. If it is she who has died, the effect will be greater. The baby will sense something terrible has happened, but they must be helped interpret this in a way they can understand.

Pre-verbal children will be particularly affected by the behaviour and attitude of those around them. As this may be their first experience of death, it will remain with them for life.

This is not to say it is wrong to show emotion, especially to cry in front of babies or small children. It is actually very important that their first experience of death is allied with the experience of adults grieving 'well'.

They therefore learn 'from the cradle' that it is OK for adults, including men, to cry and be sad. They also need to see adults stop crying and carry on with their normal life.

In early years, i.e. the first two or so, children's learning of attachment and separation and sense of security is established for life. This can be seriously shaken or affected by the death of the mother, main carer, father or other close adult or sibling. In the tragic event of the death of the mother of a small child, everything possible should be done to keep a continuity of care and carer, and also of familiar places and things. Adults and older siblings should try to restrain fearful and panic-like behaviour around the small child.

As children get older they gradually begin to understand death. Toddlers can see death as temporary, that the deceased will come back after a time. Later, around school age, they begin to ask difficult questions. From the age of about ten, children begin to realise their own mortality and the inevitability of death for all humans. This may lead to a lot of anxiety, especially if one parent or sibling has died already. They may fear that others may follow. This is particularly common when the deaths have been sudden.

Questions

Generally speaking, children will ask all they want and need to know about the whole subject of death, dying and bereavement. That is, unless they pick up or sense that it is a taboo subject in the family. As there is a lot of denial in our society, which results in taboo, older children will probably have picked it up outside the home from peers, media, etc.

The way to deal with questions is:

- Always answer the question.
- Always tell the truth.
- Never answer more than the question implies, unless you strongly sense the child is really asking more than they are able to verbalise.

Always answer

No child who is old enough to ask a question is too young to get an answer. If they ask at a very awkward time, tell them you'll answer it later, 'at such and such a time', and be sure to go back to it at that time. They may need a little attention from you when you do answer, so wait until you have some space in your day. If they repeatedly ask the same question, remember that it may be a different question *for them* each time, and they may not have the sophistication of language to ask it differently. Or they may be upset about the death and want attention from you about it, time to grieve with you, to talk over and over again about, for example, granddad and how much they miss him. Do not try to shield your children from death by avoiding their questions. Death is a part of life, a natural part. Don't project your fears on to them. They are resilient, intelligent and intuitive. They frequently cope much better than adults, if the subject is handled well by the adults around them.

Always tell the truth

Hiding or evading the truth or the reality, or pretending about it in some way, is the cause of great confusion for the child. If we are afraid to tell them the truth, remember it is *our* fear. Of course, what is 'truth' or 'reality'? That is a question!

As each culture and family have their own ideas about all sorts of issues – politics, sex, religion, education, etc. – and want to pass these on to their children, so they will have their ideas about dying and death and life after death, and likewise pass them on to the children. So tell them what you know and believe, as directly as you feel they are able to understand. If some of the questions seem gruesome to you, remember they may not appear so to the child.

Some children I know insisted on digging up a dead pet hamster several times to monitor the progress of its decay! It did not disturb any of them. They regarded it all in a very matter-of-fact way and took it in their stride.

Never answer more than the question

Children are usually direct and simple in their communication. If they ask questions, answer only what they have asked or, in some circumstances, what you believe them to be asking, nothing more. Do not turn the questioning into an excuse or occasion for a 'sermon', or complete explanation of the whole subject of mortality, death and the life hereafter! This is mainly because the child will usually ask exactly what she is ready or able to hear. An answer with more than she is ready for, may do damage. Secondly, she may not listen to any of it if you go on for too long!

No questions – no answers?

Some children may not ask anything. They may wish to avoid the subject altogether. This is usually because they want to deny or forget what has happened. They are afraid of the bad feelings that bringing it up will evoke in them, or they are afraid of 'breaking down'.

Give them ample time and opportunity to talk about their grief. Let them see you grieving, tell them how *you* feel occasionally and thus create the right atmosphere for them to allow themselves to grieve.

Language

Small children usually communicate simply and directly. Do the same. Do not use euphemisms when explaining or talking about death. A friend of mine's nine-year-old boy went missing for a day. When he returned home, late in the evening, his anxious and by this time angry parents asked where he had been. He said, 'I heard you say Mrs X (a neighbour) had lost her baby, so I went out looking for it in the woods!' Children can be very literal.

Try to avoid using metaphors for death like 'gone to sleep'. Children may be fearful when they, or you, go to bed that night. If you say granddad has gone to heaven, you must be prepared to explain that his body has not, where heaven is, what will he eat, if he will be hungry, why he hasn't packed his bag, brought food and clothing, etc. Be careful answering the 'why' questions. Amanda, who was about seven, and her friend were in an accident, where her friend was killed. Amanda was told God took her friend, because she was so good. Amanda worried that she hadn't been good if God hadn't taken her, and if she did become good, would she also die? What a bind for a seven-year-old!

To most of us death is a mystery, and so is life after death. Children understand and accept mystery. They also accept 'don't knows' more readily than you imagine, and more readily than adults.

Of course similes are very useful, especially comparisons between death and the seasons of nature, the leaves falling in the autumn, and flowers fading and dying after they are picked, with new life, new leaves and buds each springtime.

All this should not be confused with the symbolic language dying children use to communicate about their death and the life after.

Involving the Children

Children should be encouraged, but never forced, to participate in all the activities and rituals concerned with dying, death, the funeral and committal. None of this is inappropriate in itself for a child of any age. What can be upsetting for a child is the behaviour of some adults in these situations.

If you think you are shielding a child from pain or upset by keeping her away from any of it, you are not. You are teaching her that there is something too fearful or terrible for her to see. What she will imagine will almost certainly be far worse than any of the reality.

The child, you must remember, is also losing a grandparent, parent, sister, or brother, or whoever. She too is bereaved. Before the death, the child should be involved in looking after the dying person, or visiting them if in hospital. A small child can carry in a drink, turn the radio on, or whatever little job is appropriate to her age. All the family can, in some cases, be present when the person dies and stay with them for a time afterwards to pray, or sing to them, whatever is your custom, and grieve of course, and say goodbye.

Remember, children will learn about grieving for life from these past experiences. If they see adults crying and not falling apart, they will realise that this great healing release is acceptable and normal in such circumstances. If all the adults put on a stiff upper lip, the child will learn that that is the 'correct' thing to do.

It is important, however, that children do not spend too much time with adults who are fearful of death, mortuaries, dead bodies, funerals, burials or cremations. If you cannot be with the child yourself, or if you are very frightened, try to find a suitable adult. Find someone whose attitude to these events and rituals is accepting and open, so that they can be an example to the child and also answer her questions in a light and casual, though serious, way.

Recently, a little boy of five went to see his first dead body, that of a beloved granny, in the coffin in the church. He commented, 'She does look like granny, but she doesn't really look like granny. She's like a statue of granny. I suppose that's because her soul has gone away.' He had been well prepared. He was quite matter-of-fact. He then ran off to see all the people he knew in the church.

It is not usually a good idea to send a child away to stay with relatives or friends at this time. Small children, especially if this is their first experience of death, may imagine and worry that someone else at home will die while they are away. They may imagine that all kinds of horrible and frightening things are happening, that they must be protected from. After one loss, they are being deprived of other security 'props', such as their daily routine, familiar bed, toys, pets, etc., not to mention other family members, neighbours and their own peers and friends.

Children who do not see the remains of the deceased or attend any of the rituals, will find it all the more difficult to grieve 'well', to 'recover', get back to 'normal' living, and make new relationships.

They should be given every opportunity to say goodbye, both before the death (if possible) and in the various ways provided by ceremonies and rituals afterwards. Saying goodbye is an extremely important part of letting go, and therefore of grieving.

Listening

I have already discussed the importance of listening carefully to the questions children ask. Children also need to talk about the deceased, dying, death, life after death, their own and their parents' mortality, and many other related subjects. It is extremely important that you listen well. (See Chapter 11.) However, children need more focused attention than most adults.

Time

Children who are not asking questions, not talking and grieving, need a lot of time. Every child, in any case, needs their own special 'quality' time from one, or preferably both, parents or carers. After a death, they need it even more. When and how you plan this time depends not only on the age of the child, but when you can be free and, therefore, relaxed.

Small children often bring up fears when being tucked in at night, at bathtime, if they wake up after a nightmare, or first thing in the morning.

Older children might open up more easily out fishing, walking, playing scrabble, or on a visit to McDonald's!

All children may need encouragement to talk out their fears and grief. You, their parents or carers, will know best how and when to do that.

Counselling and Therapy

Parents and carers often ask how they can judge if a child needs professional counselling. The signs that a child is 'in trouble' after a bereavement are quite similar to those in adults, but of course some are different. The main signs are disturbed sleep or bad nightmares, lack of concentration and poor school grades, certain repeating illnesses, under- or over-eating, anxiety, exaggerated attention-seeking, anger and school phobia. If any of these persist, it may be due to the effect of the bereavement on the child, or there may be another cause.

If any of the above are happening to your child, you, with perhaps some advice from her teacher or your doctor, are the best judge of how to handle the situation. It is quite normal for children to act out their distress about the death of someone they loved. It is the degree of this acting out, how long it persists, and how you are able to handle it, that must determine if you wish to seek professional help. Certainly, before you do this, try encouraging the child to talk to you, giving her time on her own with you, as described previously. Also, it may be useful to have family meetings, or less formal times together as a family, to reminisce and to grieve. More of this in Chapter 12 on ritual.

Children express a lot of their grieving through play, especially by re-enacting the trauma they have been through, sometimes over and over again.

If, having done all you can to help the child yourself, there are still major problems, you may decide to seek outside help. Sometimes the child's teacher or doctor may be sufficient, depending on the way the child is behaving.

If you wish to consult a professional therapist or counsellor, or maybe have the child join a group specially for bereaved children, use the same guidelines as for selecting a therapist or counsellor for yourself (see Chapter 10).

In the case of an older child, the school guidance counsellor may be of great assistance, either herself or in recommending someone.

If you are attending a therapist or counsellor yourself, you may be able to deal there with how your child's behaviour is affecting you, and how to help her. That may be sufficient.

Children's Ways of Coping

Play

One of the main ways children cope or deal with grief is through play, just as they work out a lot of other problems and fears this way. It is their form of therapy, and you should encourage them. Often they will re-enact illness, playing doctors and nurses, funerals, etc., without any prompting. Don't be alarmed if they repeat these rituals over and over again, even months or years after the event.

If they are not doing it in this way, and if you feel they are not coping well with the death and grieving, you could spend time playing with them. If you suggest playing with small children after a bereavement, they will eventually (maybe not immediately) suggest games connected in some way to the illness, death or funeral. When they do, allow them to create the scene and lead you in their game. Agree with anything they suggest, go along with whatever they want you to do. This is their therapy.

This also helps them to cope with feelings of helplessness associated with death. It particularly helps with children's first experience of it. They can have power now over what happens, in the re-enactment, and power over you adults!

Pets

The death of a beloved pet is very often a child's first brush with death. Do not underestimate their grief. A pet can be a true friend (and not only to a child) and must be grieved. Also this dying, death and surrounding ritual will act as a model, in a way, for all future deaths, and for the child's attitude to death, dying and grieving.

Allow the child to be with the pet while it is dying. Once again, don't try to shield her. When the pet has died, allow her to cry and grieve in whatever way she wishes. Join her if you can. You can then have a wake if you wish, that is, lay out the pet for other children, family and friends to come and say goodbye.

Have a 'proper' funeral if you are able to bury the pet yourselves in the garden or wherever. If you cannot do this, do your best to dispose of it in as dignified a way as possible.

If the pet dies at the vet's, ask the vet can you be with it or see it after it has died. If you are on a farm, your children may be more accustomed to animals coming and going, but they also have pets, with whom the relationship is special.

If a pet dies after a death in the family, it can help children to grieve for the relative also. Recently, a child I knew died. Her small seven-year-old brother Johnny had a goldfish and it died about three months later. Johnny 'went to town' on the funeral. He carefully lined a matchbox with silk, as he had seen his sister's coffin. The whole family attended an elaborate ritual and burial in the garden, all masterminded and directed by Johnny. He made a special grave and stone with 'Goldie Ryan' inscribed. It seemed to help him.

Comparing Experiences

Some children, particularly only children, who are bereaved, derive great comfort from meeting, sharing experiences with, or reading of other children who have had similar experiences. It helps with the feelings of denial, isolation and loneliness. I often recommend *How It Feels When A Parent Dies* by Jill Krementz, either to children to read themselves or to parents. It is a series of accounts, written by children themselves, of the experience of a parent's death.

One child I know, Susanne, wrote her story for me. I was greatly honoured by her trusting me sufficiently to give it to me, and to allow me to include it in this book. I have reproduced it exactly as it was written. I think it helped Susanne in the difficult process of coming to terms with her beloved Daddy's death:

> I have lots of memories of my dad. One time I went camping with him when Jean was at camp. I have lots of pitchers of him. He was a scout. I am in the Irish Girl Guides. Now I hate answering the phone because one time about three months ago a man asked for my dad. I said I'll get my Mum. My Dad died when I was six years old. We were on holidays, he was up mt blonk a big bolder hit his sholder and brok his neck. Jean was unwell when we went home. I just went to my room. My Granny and my Nanna and my Anty was there. They gave us lots of gudys, that did not make up for daddy. My daddys brother was there too. I went up to our gold fish pond. Our daddy made it. I have one good frend in school. She is never too 'hello Susanne are you all right' or not nice to me her name is Alice we are pen pals and school pals too. Our budgies flew away the next year. This year we got cockateils. My dad had a twin sister her children are 9 and 12 there names are Rachel is 12 and Mark is 9 (I think). My god mother is like a 2nd daddy to me I like her a lot. My sister is very nice to me. Some times she is not. My mummy is really nice too. I want to know why it was Him. I want him here now. I realy want daddy.
>
> *Susanne – Aged 8*

Ritual

I will be devoting a whole chapter to ritual, but here I would like to address the subject of children specifically, in the rituals surrounding dying, death, committal and remembrance.

As I have said before, children can and should be involved in all the grieving rituals, but not forced. However, they can be encouraged and asked to join in, in ways that help them to overcome any fears they may have. As a ten-year-old, I was asked starkly, 'Do you want to go to your father's funeral?' Being already traumatised and frightened by his sudden death, and having never been to a funeral before (that I can remember), I said no. If someone had explained what would happen and reassured me I would be with a friend or friends (as my mother appeared to me to be too grief-stricken to be any support), I think I would have gone, and my grieving for him would have been made so much easier.

After the fuss has died down and the main rituals are over, children can still be helped to grieve, and adults too, by putting aside specific times to remember the one who has died. Children often create their own rituals naturally. Little Johnny, whom I mentioned before, regularly visits his sister's grave on his own, saying 'I'm going up to Susie's'. He buys a packet of crisps on the way. He stands in front of the grave solemnly eating the crisps, then walks round and round the grave still eating the crisps, talking to Susan until they are finished. This is his own ritual.

In their home, Johnny is specially 'in charge' of Susan's room. She was a young teenager whose room is full of posters and memorabilia she had collected. He takes care of all this and is very proud of his role. It is his way of remembering a very special sister. Incidentally, Johnny, of all the family, is getting on with his own life best and accepting Susan's sudden death.

Remembering

We all have different ways of remembering those who have died. Remembering can be very painful at first, but I feel it is a 'sweet sorrow'. Later, memories are a wonderful gift.

For children, events like the death of a loved one are a really important part of their character and personality formation. It is helpful for them to have memories kept alive, through ritual, photographs, anniversaries and in other ways.

However, their lives must not be made gloomy, maudlin, or morbid. Children, like adults, have to get on with living and eventually 'let go'. A balance can be kept with occasional and appropriate 'memorials' at times such as Christmas, birthdays and other anniversaries.

Another little boy I know, Brian, always brings something belonging to his beloved dead sister with him on special occasions. He wore her socks for his First Communion. Children are very creative and will invent not only their own ways of remembering, but of grieving, letting go and getting on with their lives.

PART IV

HELP FOR THE JOURNEY

CHAPTER 10

GRIEF COUNSELLING AND GRIEF THERAPY

When Counselling or Therapy May be Needed

Grieving is not a dis-ease. The dis-ease occurs rather when you do not grieve. Grieving actually eases the pain. When your innate healing mechanisms have not been conditioned or damaged, you will grieve naturally, if not interfered with, and recover eventually, in the right conditions and environment.

When, then, might you need to go to a counsellor or psychotherapist? The first thing I would say is, if you feel you would like to go, then do so. Discuss the problem with the therapist, check out what you want and expect, and see if she is able to meet those expectations. It is important to understand that it is you who must do the grieving, not the therapist. The therapist will not be doing anything *for* you, but simply acting as a guide or facilitator for your grieving.

If you do not have sufficient support from friends and family, you may want to get some professional help. In order to give good support, listeners need to have some 'free attention' for you. If they also are grieving, their attention will be involved with their own grief and there will not be enough left for you. Friends, outside the family or close circle, are often most helpful. But if you are not fortunate enough to have such friends, or enough of them, or if they are involved in the situation, you may need a professional grief counsellor or therapist.

If the death you are grieving has been particularly violent or distressing, you may need professional help. Again it is a question of free attention. Few non-professionals are able to listen at length to the details of certain illnesses and deaths, such as AIDS, suicide or murder. If you have been bereaved in such a way, you may need to talk over your experience again and again. Listening to your experience may just be too much for some people, even the most supportive of friends. Listening may remind them of their own squeamishness or fears, and hence their free attention goes to themselves and away from you.

In his book, *Grief Counselling & Grief Therapy*, William Worden writes of 'normal' and 'abnormal' grief reactions, 'complicated' and 'uncomplicated' grieving and 'pathological' grief. This suggests a black-and-white approach, with a definite dividing line between the 'normal'/'uncomplicated' and the 'abnormal'/'complicated' and 'pathological'. I prefer to see it as a continuum, with each person's way of grieving at a different point along this line.

Trust yourself as to whether you wish to go to a professional. The time element is of the utmost importance. Certain grief reactions that are usual early on may not be 'normal' if still occurring four years later. If you are still undecided, use the following checklist:

• Six weeks to three months after your bereavement, are you unable to get back to what was 'normal' work?

• Have you become addicted to non-prescribed drugs, alcohol or other substances or behaviour since your bereavement?

• Are you 'hyperactive' to the point of suffering extreme fatigue or insomnia?

• Are you experiencing serious physical symptoms, which you or your doctor connect to your bereavement in any way?

• Have you what you consider to be an 'abnormal' fear of dying yourself, or of the type of illness of which your loved one died?

• Are you experiencing clinical depression? If in doubt, consult your doctor.

• Do you at any time seriously consider suicide?

If you answer a definite 'yes' to any one of these questions, you could consider professional help.

However, writing as a therapist, I think that consulting a professional could help a bereaved person who is simply lonely and finding life difficult or unbearable.

Choosing a Counsellor or Therapist

Personally, I believe there is a difference between 'counselling' and 'psychotherapy'. Counselling focuses mainly on the problem or symptom and ends usually in six to twelve months maximum, when that problem or symptom has been 'resolved'. I would look upon psychotherapy as a deeper process, probably continuing over a longer period, and including focus on the self, early development, and possibly with a spiritual (not necessarily religious) aspect.

However, the two processes are very closely linked and many people do not make the distinction, and use the two terms interchangeably to mean exactly the same thing. Psychotherapists, generally speaking, have had a longer training. It is important to establish that the person you choose has appropriate qualifications and standing.

Studies show that what influences the effectiveness of counselling or therapy is the quality of the relationship between client and counsellor or therapist, not the technique used or philosophical stance of the practitioner. This would bear out my insistence that it is the client who does the work, not the counsellor or therapist.

Generally speaking, in grief counselling the main focus is on one particular loss, and possibly other losses that have been re-stimulated by that particular one. Often the loss is quite recent, though not always.

When you experience a major loss, you come to it with your whole being and past history, positive and negative. Therefore the way you cope is dependent on who you are at this time. If there are serious or unresolved problems in your personality, or from your past, these will emerge as you endeavour to cope. Again, speaking generally, these unresolved issues, if causing problems, should be looked at with a trained psychotherapist who is experienced in grief work.

Grief counsellors can be people who have done part-time training of some kind, often connected with their work as a nurse, priest, parish worker, or worker in a voluntary counselling agency. Some agencies run their own training courses. However, some are fully-trained professional counsellors.

The very best way to find a grief counsellor or therapist is to get personal recommendation. Of course, different therapists suit different people and different clients have different expectations. For a good personal recommendation, ask friends or relatives, or professionals such as social workers or clergy, for their recommendations.

Some professional bodies provide lists of accredited counsellors or psychotherapists. Choose one who lists grief as a speciality. Some people prefer a therapist who lives locally, others prefer to travel in an attempt to ensure anonymity.

Check them out

Do not hesitate to check out a counsellor or therapist. Some will count this as a session and charge you, but it is well worth it even if they do. Ideally this is someone whom you should be able to trust in a relatively short time, someone with whom you will very soon develop an intimate relationship of sorts. Ask as many questions as you wish. Do not be afraid to ask anything. Tell the counsellor your needs and expectations.

Cost

The cost of counselling and therapy varies enormously. Some voluntary organisations provide free counselling. At the other end of the scale, you can pay a full consultant psychiatrist's fee (a percentage of which may be refundable on health insurance).

Some professionals, such as social workers and other healthcare professionals, provide counselling or psychotherapy at no charge to the client. The amount you are asked to pay is not always in proportion to the value of the service rendered.

Confidentiality

Professional counsellors and therapists are bound by strict codes of professional conduct and can usually be trusted to keep your session absolutely confidential. If this worries you, ask them about it.

When you are involved in group therapy, it is more difficult to ensure confidentiality. If you are concerned, ask the group leader or bring it up in the group.

Remember, a lot of grieving can be done without revealing any intimate details about yourself.

For how long?

If you decide to engage in grief counselling or psychotherapy, the process usually lasts for anything from one to two sessions to a period of years. Most counsellors or psychotherapists will see you once a week, some twice a week, initially at least. Some will reduce it to once a fortnight after a time.

It is common to make a contract with your counsellor or therapist for a certain number of sessions. At the end of that number, you and the counsellor or therapist can review progress, and renew the contract for a further period, if agreed. I find this helpful. It puts a structure on the process, and helps you to identify 'progress'.

Individual versus group counselling or therapy

Like the choice of a counsellor or therapist, the choice between individual or group counselling or therapy is often made on personal recommendation. Again, different types of therapy suit different people. Many people, while grieving, engage in both the individual and group processes, either concurrently or one after the other.

Trust is an important part of the therapeutic relationship. If you think this may be difficult for you, perhaps you should begin with individual counselling or therapy.

I believe that each process has its own particular richness to offer, and its own strengths.

Both individuals and group counsellors and psychotherapists vary in their approach and techniques. It would be impossible to cover all of them here.

If you decide on a specific counsellor or therapist or group, and after a few sessions feel like leaving or ending the process, discuss it with the counsellor or therapist before leaving.

This kind of work on yourself, often intense, can evoke all kinds of feelings from deep within you. They may have nothing to do with the rationalisations you may be engaging in, or using as a way out of the situation. As you have read in Chapter 6, many of the feelings associated with grief, such as anger, guilt, fear, etc., can be experienced as unpleasant, and you may want to give up and bury them again. Do not do that without careful consideration.

Support Groups

Bereavement groups and support groups are springing up everywhere. It is heartening to see the spread of interest in bereavement, and the willingness of people to help those who are grieving.

If you join such a group, ask beforehand what is on offer, and check against your expectations.

Usually such groups are not therapeutically oriented, though they may provide healing experiences for members. What I mean by this is that they don't usually have a professional counsellor or therapist to engage in individual counselling or therapy, or to facilitate group therapy.

If you are expecting support from group members outside of session time, check if this is part of the agreement of all members. Be sure to get all of the boundaries and agreements clear beforehand. Then you have much less possibility of being disappointed.

Residential Workshops

Some therapists or therapy and counselling centres offer residential workshops, usually lasting for anything from two days to a week.

At some such workshops, the main work is done in a large group or several small groups using some form of group therapy.

Residential workshops usually use a variety of media or techniques such as meditation, art work, music and singing, play, guided imagery, inner child work and group sharing.

The great advantage of these workshops is that they provide a vehicle to give people a particular kind of opportunity to work through their grief, or whatever the relevant issue happens to be for them.

Such workshops complement their weekly or regular therapy sessions, whatever their theoretical orientation. They do not interfere with regular therapy. They can be seen as a resource not only for participants, but for therapists to recommend to their clients.

These workshops allow participants a more intense experience than is possible in weekly therapy. People can stay with their feelings or process for long periods in a really safe environment.

An important part of the process is the integration of whatever unfolding has taken place within the individual, into their own daily living. Much time and consideration is given to helping participants to 'ground' themselves, and return home ready to face back into their 'normal' life.

CHAPTER ELEVEN

What Can I Do? Helping the Bereaved

How Can I Help?

Throughout this book I have put a lot of emphasis on the importance of the bereaved person asking for help to have their needs met. There are several reasons for this, among them:

1. People are so unique that everyone's individual needs are quite different.
2. Asking for help is a contradiction of the feeling of helplessness and powerlessness that death so often evokes. If the bereaved person is able to ask, then you must answer according to how much you can willingly give, without seriously damaging yourself or your family. 'Love you neighbour as yourself.'

However, there are some individuals who, for some reason or other, just cannot ask. If you have a bereaved friend or relative who is in this position, you may wish to help in some way without being asked. Try to check that it is not a case of genuinely not wanting any help, or having enough already.

Embarrassment

Most people experience a lot of embarrassment with regard to the whole issue of death and dying – besides all the other feelings. That is one of the reasons why so many jokes centre on death, funerals, churchyards, corpses, ghosts, etc. Laughing helps to dispel the embarrassment, and the fear too.

We often use excuses to avoid bereaved people, funerals, burials, etc., because of our embarrassment. How often have you heard (or said yourself), 'It's a time for the family to be together', or 'I don't want to intrude'?

Of course, there are occasions when this is true, but they are much more rare than you imagine. Most families welcome close friends' sympathy and support. If in doubt, ask. Be sensitive. At a large funeral, the bereaved may not notice everyone who is there. Paradoxically, they will always remember those who were not! Families and local customs vary regarding attendance at the cremation or burial. I believe it is not customary to go back to the family house afterwards, unless invited.

Visiting in the weeks following the death can be supportive, but it can also be very tiring for the family if there is a constant stream of visitors to be entertained. Short visits are the most helpful, and suggesting that the family telephone if they would like you to come again or to help in any other way.

The only way I know to overcome embarrassment is to feel it, and do whatever needs to be done *through* the feelings. It can help to talk it over beforehand. If you only knew how much a word, or a hug, or a handshake can help! I don't know how many times I have crossed roads to avoid a bereaved person out of embarrassment. That was before I was bereaved. If you don't know what to say, say nothing – a touch or a loving, warm expression are marvellous ways of communicating. If you are afraid you may cry, don't stop your tears. They too are great communicators. Sharing tears together for someone you both loved can be tremendously healing and comforting.

Because of our embarrassment, I always suggest erring on the side of involvement rather than staying away. If families want privacy, they usually put 'funeral or house private' in the death notice, which of course you must respect. However, I have discovered that some families say that, not intending it for close friends. Again, ask.

Practical Help

Like everything connected with bereavement, the way in which you can be of practical assistance varies according to the person and their circumstances. Be careful not to take away their power to make their own decisions. That does not mean they have to do everything themselves.

The ideal situation, I believe, is for those most closely bereaved to conduct the orchestra of helpers. Especially in the days around the death, funeral and committal, there are many practical tasks to be undertaken. Some are related directly to the death and funeral arrangements, others to seeing that the ordinary tasks of life go on as normally as possible, such as providing food, house maintenance, caring for children and elderly people, even taking the dog for a walk.

If there is a large extended family, they usually rally round, but not always. If the bereaved person is elderly or living alone, there are many more ways in which you can help. The loneliest time is after a few weeks, when the fuss and excitement has died down. Even a year later, when the first anniversary has passed, it can be very lonely, as everyone expects the bereaved person to be 'over it'. Re-engaging in life without a loved one, especially a partner, is a very difficult and lonely task. It is a time when most people could use a little help from their friends.

While the bereaved person is numb with shock, especially following a sudden death, they may need most things done for them. But it is often good for them to start taking some decisions as soon as this stage has passed. Decision-making means decision-making, not necessarily carrying out the task.

Some tasks, too, are difficult for certain people, for example, coping with tax issues for some or working the washing machine for others. Practical advice and help can be invaluable.

Listening

Listening to a bereaved person telling their story is one of the ways in which you can be most helpful. If you were also close to the person who died, this may be difficult for you, but don't feel guilty about it. Bereaved people need a number of listeners and supporters. Give what time you can without exhausting yourself to the point where *you* too begin to need help.

Many people are 'natural' listeners, and some seem to be 'natural' talkers. We can all learn to listen well though. There are some skills you can develop to help you listen better, and I will list them, and give a few guidelines to make it a little easier. However, the most important skill is to be yourself. Genuineness comes across, and most of us know instinctively, in fact immediately, if someone is really listening, really interested, or pretending.

Attention

I talked about listening in Chapter 1, and how easy it is to be tempted to jump in with our own 'story'. Attention is a simple concept. If I am preoccupied with my own problems, whether it be a toothache, the roast in danger of burning in the oven, a row I have just had with my husband, or my mother dying of cancer, I cannot give all my attention to listening. Part of it is being drawn to whatever my preoccupation is. So just listen, for as long as your attention can focus on your friends. You can help to make the attention-span longer by talking to someone else about *your* problem, or, if possible, solving it in a practical way, if it is that type of problem. Remember that hurtful things, which may have happened many years ago, can also pull our attention away from listening.

Quiet

Many conversations are a competition between two or more people for each other's attention. As soon as one has drawn breath, the other comes in with their own similar experience. While each is talking, the other's 'buttons are being pressed', and they are focusing on how to talk about their *own* experience rather than listening, giving attention to the person who is recounting *their* story.

It's not easy to remain quiet and, literally, 'keep your mouth shut'. Practise it in any conversation you are having, and you may be surprised how quickly you will feel compelled to interrupt.

It is occasionally comforting to know that the person you are talking to has been through a similar experience, that they 'understand'. But this can be communicated with a simple phrase like, 'I know. I've been through it myself', or 'I remember that part so well', or whatever. What they do not need to hear is the details of your story. Trust me on that, the temptation can be very strong. It is a difficult tightrope to walk, between quiet and pretence.

Giving advice

As I have mentioned before, do not give advice unless asked, and even then, be slow about it. Remember, people seldom take your advice anyway, and they usually do what they wanted to do in the first place.

Interest

It is usually not difficult to be interested the first time you hear a story. The tenth time is a different matter. There is no magic answer to staying interested and being genuine. Being genuine is what matters most. Looking after yourself helps, that is, by not listening for too long at a time, and only listening when you are rested and have lots of free attention and not too many of your own problems.

Asking questions to draw the person out, to elaborate on their story and to tell pieces they did not tell before, can help both listener and talker. If some of what you are listening to appears to you to be violent, gruesome, gory or very upsetting (and this is really an individual matter), having someone else to unload to can help.

A lot of us, particularly healthcare professionals, tend to have a detective-type attitude to listening. We tend to collect facts, piece together a picture or story, decide on a solution, and then feed that solution back to the speaker in the form of advice. There are, of course, occasions when that is useful, but when someone is bereaved, and particularly in the first year or so, what they usually need is listening only – simply listening.

Confidentiality

A bereaved person grieving with a friend usually takes a certain amount of confidentiality for granted. Can you guarantee them this? This safety is of the utmost importance, especially in a small town or country area. If you break this, you break a kind of unspoken sacred bond, and that bond can never be repaired.

If, as I have recommended, *you* need to 'unload' to someone else, in order to be a better listener yourself, either choose a professional counsellor/therapist or someone you feel you can really trust. In either case, state your requirements in regard to confidentiality, quite specifically.

Respect/Acceptance

You might wonder why I include respect. Of course you respect your friend! Yes, but do you accept all her ideas, her views and her lifestyle? Do you accept her ways of dealing with death, dying and bereavement, her way of coping with grieving? It can be difficult, especially if the bereaved person comes from a different race, religion, culture, tradition or class than you do. You are there to listen, to help her take her own power in a situation where that is very difficult, not to advise or give your opinion. She doesn't (almost certainly) want to know how *you* would do it in your family or country or Church. Occasionally, of course, this can be helpful. We all need to move out a little from old traditions, try new things, but it must feel right for the people closely involved. It may not feel *familiar*, but it must feel right, and they do not necessarily go hand in hand.

Can you have enough acceptance, tolerance and compassion to listen to someone whose loved one has died of AIDs, or has killed themselves, or who has had an abortion? If you know you just could not manage to listen to such a person well, do not take it on. Or just listen to a small part of how they are feeling, and find someone with whom you can work out your prejudices.

Empathy

To show real empathy with a grieving person is treading another tightrope, this time between over-identifying or over-involvement and so losing attention, and cold detachment. I have already focused a lot on over-identifying, and it is on that side that most of us tend to err.

Sometimes, however, if you have been a main support person for a bereaved friend, and are beginning to get 'burnt out', you may find yourself, almost unconsciously, detaching yourself and 'hardening your heart'. Understandable as this is, it is of little help to your friend. This is the time to 'bow out' for a period, take a rest, go away for a weekend. Find some ways to recharge your batteries.

'Tea and sympathy' is something we all need at times, and isn't that one of the things friends are for? However, be careful not to confuse this with listening in a way that is enabling your friend to grieve. Tea, coffee, alcohol, cigarettes or food are 'comforting'; they are frequently used to suppress feelings, and, of course, some of them are actually a danger to our health – all, if not taken in moderation. All the myriad acts that go to make up what we call friendship, can be so very, very healing, and none should be extolled over another. But, once again, remember the balance.

Time

Individuals differ very much, and they grieve to their own pattern and rhythm. That is the most important thing to remember about time. The other is not to wean down your time commitment too soon, and remember, time as we conceive it is a human concept. When in pain or grieving a loved one, a minute can be like an hour, and two or three years like so many days. This, of course, can pose problems for friends and helpers of all kinds.

Touch

Some families are 'touchy families', some are not. If yours is, remember that not everyone's is. Again, embarrassment plays an important part. If in doubt, ask, for example, 'Would you like a hug?' Don't be upset if the answer is negative, we all have different physical boundaries. When a grieving person is crying, a gentle arm round their shoulder, or on the knee or hand, can be comforting. It can, in some cases, stop them crying. So, be sensitive; watch for reaction.

Occasionally, we touch people when they are crying in order to make *ourselves* feel better. We hate to see someone, especially a friend, in pain or suffering, and we long to do *something*. In this compulsive longing, we forget it is good for them to cry, and we reach out in our need to be of help. Watch out for that.

Religion/Spirituality

If you have religious or spiritual beliefs that you think may be of help to the bereaved person, be sensitive in introducing them. If they are in tune with your friend's way of thinking, they can be of immense comfort and consolation. I often explain this aspect of listening by asking, for example, 'Do you have a belief in life after death?' or 'Do you think you mother can still be in touch with you?' or 'Do you find prayer helpful?', etc. That way, you can open up the subject for discussion. Try to use interventions on *their* themes of religion or spirituality to console, rather than yours. At some stage, you may find an appropriate space to recount how religion or a sense of spirituality helped you (if it did). New ideas are important, but just think – are you saying this for their comfort or your own?

Nowadays, people often feel shy or reticent in admitting that they would like religious or spiritual guidance from a priest or minister of their religion. If you sense this may help, ask them. Also, do not be shy or reticent yourself in discussing such things, and offer such comfort and consolation. After all, 'There is that of God in everyone' (George Fox).

The self and creativity

By this, I mean just use yourself, all that you are, your whole being, made up of what has gone to make you who you are. Use the wonderful creative being that is you, to be present for your friend in whatever way you can serve her best. You can get ideas from this book, from the many other books written on the subject, from talking to individuals, from listening to professionals, and from all your life experiences.

Above all, though, when you have taken in and digested all these, it is the spirit in you that will shine through, with the light that heals.

Taking Care of Yourself

In order to allow this healing light to shine through, you have to keep yourself in good shape. Some people might say you have to 'keep your channel clear'. According to our upbringing, culture, traditions and beliefs, and most of all because of our own uniqueness, we have different ways of doing this. You need to give attention to body, mind, emotions and spirit. You should try to be in good physical, mental, emotional and spiritual shape, primarily for your *own* sake.

CHAPTER TWELVE

THE PLACE OF RITUAL

Ritual plays a vital part in the grieving process. The main rituals designed for grieving by the various Churches take place very early on in the process, usually in the first week after the death. These rituals follow familiar patterns. This familiarity is comforting and gives us a feeling of security and continuity, important for those early days of grieving. Some people, though, are so deeply involved in their private grief that they only participate to a limited degree, or are almost completely unaware of what is going on. It is important, however, to attend all of these rituals, if you can, and to participate as fully as you are able. But don't push yourself too much.

Later on, you may feel you missed out. You may have been ill or unable to attend for any number of reasons. Or you may have been physically present, but too upset or distracted to be mentally and emotionally present.

In some cases, as with a person missing and presumed dead, or an aborted foetus, there is no funeral ritual or burial ceremony.

If, for any reason at all, you feel you have not marked the death of your loved one in the symbolic way that ritual allows, and that you would like to, you can, alone or with the help of others, create your own ritual. Remember, it is never too late. This chapter is intended to help you to do that. It is also intended to help you to contribute more to, and participate more fully in, the rituals provided by the various churches, particularly the rituals for death and burial.

It seems that ritual must include:

- repetition or routine
- symbolic meaning
- the marking of some specific event
- physical elements, such as words and actions.

If you want to participate fully in rituals that others have created, or to contribute to them, change them or create your own, it is important to think about each of these components. You can create and participate in all kinds of rituals to help you to heal the pain of grief, and grow from the experience. There are rituals you create naturally, almost without realising it, like putting notices in the paper to announce the death and to thank people who have supported you in your grief. Other rituals are major events in which you participate, created usually by the various Churches, like funeral and burial services. But whether big or small, public or private, they are always markers of bigger events in your personal journey.

We tend to think of rituals as these major formal ceremonies, organised by other people, which we may participate in or simply observe. Many rituals have ceased to have any deep significance or meaning for us. We often take part 'in automatic'. We often see the ritual as significant in itself, rather than an outward material symbol marking the deeper meaning of inner changes in our lives or our beings. This symbolism is the one element that all rituals have in common, and which I believe defines and differentiates ritual from other events – it allows us to find meaning in what may appear to be very ordinary or mundane.

If you think about it, was it not the significance of the event that made it memorable? Remember the children's birthday party. It wasn't, for example, simply the food and the people who gathered that made it a ritual. It was the whole occasion, marking the birth of a new family member and another year in her life. This ritual probably comprised some or all of the following:

- A number of people gathered specifically for the occasion, probably dressed in party clothes.
- Shared communal food, including one type of food traditionally present at this type of ritual – a decorated cake.
- Lighted candles on the cake, one for each year of the child's life.
- Singing a traditional song, one that is always sung on such occasions, 'Happy Birthday to You'.
- Bringing and giving of gifts to the central figure of the ritual.

Some communities and families add their own particular touch, which after some years becomes an important part of the whole ritual, for example, an extra song or speech by some family member.

Similarly with a funeral service:

- People, and especially family mourners, often wear black or sombre clothes.
- There is a religious service. This, a ritual within a ritual, involves all kinds of symbolism, including many ways of acknowledging the death of the deceased, the loss for the relatives and friends, and the transition to another form of existence.
- People bring flowers, letters and cards.
- They gather to shake hands and talk to the bereaved and reminisce about the deceased.
- They accompany (and frequently walk with) the remains to wherever they are to be laid to rest.
- Some of the people may adjourn to a pub, hotel or the family home to share food and drink.

The death of someone close is one of the most significant changes we ever experience in our lifetime. It is one of the many different types of hurdles life seems to erect in our pathway. We can choose to allow the experience to block us from continuing on the journey, or we can find ways to climb over. But we cannot deny it, ignore it, or pretend that it is not there. That leads to stagnation at best, and pain, depression, illness and despair at worst. These hurdles, painful as they are to deal with, are important turning points on our particular unique pathway.

While we are climbing over the particular hurdles (when we are grieving), or when we have reached the other side (when our grieving is complete), we can integrate and learn from the experience. One of the ways in which we can be facilitated to do this is through the medium of ritual. It is a vital part of grief work.

Many books have been written on the subject of ritual: ethnic and religious, public and private, some specifically focusing on rituals connected with grieving, death, transition and transformation.

There seem to be as many definitions of the word 'ritual' as there are individual rituals. Carl Jung believed that we humans have an inbuilt need to acknowledge the 'supra-mundane', i.e. what is more than ordinary, that which is beyond or underlying the usual everyday events we call 'reality'. Ritual is a word that can conjure up all kinds of events in our past, both happy and sad. When you think about it, our memories are studded with occasions that involve ritual – births, christenings, circumcisions, first communions, confirmations, bat and bar mitzvahs, birthdays, graduations, presentations, family meals and celebrations, Christmases and other holidays, weddings and, of course, funerals and shivas.

When you recall these events and what they had in common, you can discover for yourself what constitutes ritual.

Repetition and routine

This can be repetition of the whole ritual in the same circumstances, for example, a party with cake and candles each time there is a birthday, or a blessing or procession with similar words and actions each time a christening or marriage ceremony is performed.

Another type of repetition is when certain actions and words are repeated within the one ritual, for example, the repetition of words in various blessings or prayers within a funeral service.

Symbolic meaning

Meaning is something that each individual, with their own unique past experiences, takes from certain images, music, words or actions. 'Our song' for one person has no meaning for another. The Sign of the Cross, Star of David or a religious icon carry particular history and meaning for some, but none for others, depending on their particular religion or culture.

Marking an event

This may seem obvious: birthday parties mark birthdays, and funerals, death. However, not all rituals mark events in such an obvious way. For example, the reason Christians mark Christmas is often forgotten. Funerals not only mourn the passing, and celebrate the life, of the deceased, but they also mark the beginning of the separation and letting go process for the bereaved.

Physical elements

All rituals contain physical elements appropriate to the occasion and its meaning. Because ritual is about symbolism and meaning, it plays an important part in attempting to give meaning to events like death, which can seem meaningless and unexplainable. It usually includes articles that are universally regarded as symbolic, but you should include those that have meaning for you or the deceased.

All the rituals we are concerned with here involve humans, made up of body, mind, emotions and spirit, inhabiting this physical universe. The meaning we are giving, or trying to give, to the occasion is in this context. It is customary, therefore, to include in a ritual articles, words and actions that evoke aspects of humanness and of all that constitutes our universe. Many also include symbols invoking God.

If you wish to create your own ritual, the following is an extensive checklist you can choose from when you are planning it.

To represent humanness – The senses

Sound	Music, songs, hymns, psalms, poems, wise sayings and other quotations
Sight	Colour, shape, things from nature, light and darkness, special clothes
Smell	Incense, oils, food, drinks
Taste	Food, drinks, oils, salt
Touch	Blessing, anointing, hugging, kissing, touching hands, washing

To represent the universe

Time	Division of the time allocated for the ritual in various ways
Space	Creation of a sacred space in which the ritual is held, for example, the altar in a church, or a designated area in a room, marked by a circle of chairs. North, south, east and west can be acknowledged by facing in a particular direction,

or by verbally acknowledging them, as the altar in a Christian church normally faces east.

Elements

Earth   Sprinkling, digging
Fire   Lighting of fire or use of candles
Water   Washing, pouring, drinking
Air   Breathing in and out – as in meditation
Metal   Use of precious metals, e.g. gold and silver

Ritual has been used as far back as we know, to mark all kinds of events in the life of the tribe or community. As close-knit communities are rare in our society these days, ritual can perform the same function for the extended family in the event of a death.

This function includes the following:

- It formally announces the death.
- It bonds or binds together those left behind.
- It gives a sense of safety that all are joined in a single attitude to death.
- It gives support to those directly bereaved.
- It gives support to those in the wider community who are also bereaved.
- It provides an opportunity for all to grieve, albeit in public.
- It celebrates and gives thanks for the life of the deceased.
- It can be a communal act of worship.
- It marks a step in the separation and letting-go process for the bereaved.
- It can be a symbol of rebirth, transition and hope for the future.

After a death, you can participate in, or create many rituals, for example:

Just after the person dies

Praying, singing, kissing goodbye or touching, saying goodbye, laying out the remains, arranging the room and house for visitors, saying prayers together, sitting with the deceased, reminiscing and sharing memories with others.

When the remains leave the house or morgue

The remains are placed in the coffin, last prayers are said, special mementoes are put in the coffin, the coffin is closed and taken to the church, cemetery or crematorium.

When the remains arrive at the church, cemetery or crematorium

Praying, singing, sympathising, writing of names in a special book, presenting flowers, cards, letters.

Various types of funeral, burial or cremation services

These are usually provided by the Churches.

Immediately after the funeral

Family gatherings, meals, drinks, people gathering and calling to the house.

After the funeral

Reading of the will, disposing of clothes and other possessions, visiting the grave, anniversary rituals.

As I have said previously, when you are in shock or you are numb in the early stages of grief, it is most useful, and in fact necessary, for others to take overall responsibility for rituals and arrangements generally. However, within the existing ready-made ritual, you and other family members or close friends are usually free, even encouraged, to join in at certain points, to contribute ideas for the readings, music, etc. As I have said, the more you can participate and contribute, the more it will help you.

The rituals normally provided by the various Churches are very often sufficient for this part of your grieving, particularly if you can contribute something and participate fully, which often simply means no more than being able to feel part of what is going on.

Sometimes, for one reason or another, you cannot be physically present at the funeral, or in some cases there may not have been one. You may feel that you were not emotionally present, and that you 'missed' the funeral, even though you were physically present.

If you have missed a funeral in any of these ways, at a later date you may wish to create some rituals of your own to help you to grieve, integrate the experience and move on. Or you may wish to have a more formal service conducted by your Church, who are usually most willing to do this.

The following are some examples of rituals I have participated in, contributed to, created myself or with others, or that other grieving people have created. They may act as guidelines and help you to participate more fully in existing rituals or help you to create your own by yourself, or with others.

I: Participation

My mother's funeral

To put you in the picture briefly: My mother, Doreen, died suddenly in 1980 at the age of eighty-one when in apparently good health. She had had a long, full and reasonably happy life. She had been a 'convert' to Roman Catholicism from the Church of Ireland, and an art teacher of small children. She was a warm, kind and friendly person with a wide circle of friends and a keen but non-academic interest in psychology, philosophy and religion in its widest sense.

The night after she died, I met with a priest friend of ours, who was to be the chief celebrant of her funeral Mass, and a few friends, to plan the funeral. I asked if a Church of Ireland priest friend could join in concelebrating the Mass, to represent that part of my mother's life when she was a member of the Church of Ireland. At that time, the Roman Catholic Church would not allow it. After some discussion, it was agreed he could kneel at the side of the altar and participate by leading the 'Prayers of the Faithful' or 'Bidding Prayers' and by singing a solo hymn, as he had a lovely voice.

I chose three readings from the New Testament, and invited three significant people to read them.

Corinthians 12:4-13

I asked Helen, a Roman Catholic friend of my mother's, to read this. She had spent the day before my mother's death with her, working on a psychological project they were doing together.

Revelation of St John 21:1-4

I asked Risteárd, a Methodist friend of ours, of whom my mother had been very fond, to do this reading.

John 14: -4

The gospel 'In my Father's house there are many mansions' to remind us of how God loves us all (irrespective of age, creed, colour, sexuality, gender or nationality). This was read, of course, by the chief celebrant. He had prayed with my mother some months previously when she had been in hospital.

Before the funeral, the friend who had been with her when she collapsed, came with her family and decorated the church with flowers from my mother's own garden.

Offertory procession

A number of my mother's small pupils and friends brought up flowers and pictures and cards they had painted specially, besides the bread and wine.

Hymns

> 'Now Thank We All Our God' – to give thanks for a long and happy life.
> 'Christ Be With Me' – from St Patrick's Breastplate, which had been sung at my mother's Confirmation in the Church of Ireland.
> 'We Plough the Fields and Scatter' – a hymn often sung in the Church of Ireland at that time of year, Harvest Thanksgiving, a hymn of thanks for abundance.
> 'Be Thou My Vision' – one of her own favourites.

Prayers of the faithful

At this point in the ceremony, our Church of Ireland priest friend, Brian, prayed for my father, remembering his death thirty years previously, and for my Mum's sister of eighty-six, living in England and unable to be with us.

Four friends came to the altar to give thanks for particular aspects of my mother's personality: her hospitality, her teaching and gardening abilities and her rapport with young people.

Prayer

The 'Prayer after Communion' was read by a friend of mine, Pauline, who had been a frequent visitor to our home. It was about my Mum's hospitality and the ever-open door of her home. Afterwards, my friend Pauline commented:

> The event opened up for me a different way of looking at death. The preparations were very thorough and practical. There was a determination that this wonderful woman would be thought well about and honoured and, for instance, that her heritage of both the Roman Catholic and Church of Ireland faiths would be integrated into the service, which was not easy, but was very inspiring.
>
> I was asked to read a short piece. It was the first time I had ever spoken in a church, which was liberating for me as a woman. And it made me feel very close to Doreen and to her daughter, Mary Paula.
>
> The experience also helped me to organise and participate fully in my own father's funeral four years ago.

If you consider the above ritual, not many radical additions or changes were made to the conventional funeral Mass. However, each one, reflecting different aspects of my mother or her life, or ways I remembered her, resulted in a ceremony that was designed with her in mind. Consequently, I and others present felt it was a really personal 'send off' for her. This was satisfying to my sense of personal loss, my feeling that this special person had been lost to me in particular. (I am an only child and was, therefore, 'chief mourner'.)

II: Creation of a New Ritual for a Dead Baby

This was a ritual designed where there had been no other religious or community ritual. It is told with Fiona's permission.

Fiona had had an abortion three years previously. No one except her boyfriend knew. He lived a long way away, and much of their relationship had been carried on by letter. Though Fiona had now broken up with her boyfriend, Colm, she had kept many of his letters.

For her ritual of saying goodbye to her baby, at one of *Turning Point*'s workshops, Fiona decided to ask a group of people to be present as a kind of community acknowledgement and witness to the birth and life, as well as the death, of her baby, whom she named.

She chose a place beside a small tree, and we all gathered round. Some of those present had musical instruments. Fiona had brought Colm's letters with her, and a little white box, pink ribbon and a single red rose. Others also had flowers.

When we were gathered, Fiona burnt Colm's letters, making a little fire with some twigs. When cool, she put them in the little white box, tied the pink ribbon and buried it beside the tree. She laid the rose on top of the earth. She then said a few words of goodbye to the baby.

Then we played and sang the following song:

> *I have carved you in the palm of my hand*
> I will never forget you, my people
> I have carved you in the palm of my hand
> I will never forget you
> I will never forget you
> I will never forget my own
> Does a mother forget her baby?
> Or a woman, the child in her womb?
> Yet even if these forget
> Yes, even if these forget
> I will never forget my own
>
> I will never forget you, my people,
> I have carved you in the palm of my hand
> I will never forget you

I will never forget you
I will never forget my own.

Of course, it was very sad for us all, but for Fiona it was not only sad, but a turning point. It was the beginning of a new phase in her life. Now she could close the chapter of her relationship with Colm, her pregnancy, abortion and the hours of therapy that had helped her heal. She would never forget any of this, but she could move on.

Fiona says:

> After the completion of the ritual, I felt that a very heavy burden of silence had been lifted from my life. Although I felt great sadness, I also experienced the love, friendship and support of those present. In my mind, the ritual helped set my daughter's spirit free, and helped me feel whole again.

III: Creation of a New Ritual Including Scattering of Ashes

Brendan had been a healer, acupuncturist and Chinese herbalist at *Turning Point*. This ritual took place several weeks after the funeral service, for friends and relatives from abroad who were unable to attend the funeral Mass. It is told with Brendan's family's permission.

Two of us gathered ahead of time to plan the ritual. We decided that it would be divided into four parts:

1.   Welcome and Preparation
2.   Remembering Brendan
3.   Closure and Transition
4.   Scattering of Brendan's ashes

A brief programme was typed and given to people on arrival. The room was arranged with chairs around the wall and a small table at the end for special objects and the urn with his ashes.

Welcome and preparation
One person, David, who acted as MC, took responsibility for the organisation and sequence of the ritual and for explaining it to those present. He welcomed people as they arrived. I welcomed people more

formally, when all had assembled.

Certain people significant in Brendan's life, and some whom he had healed, withdrew and collected items with which they processed back into the room. They placed them on the table, which had been decorated with fruit and flowers. They brought the urn with his ashes, a photograph of Brendan, flowers, incense which he had liked to burn in his home, and a bowl of the healing herbs he had worked with.

Remembering Brendan

We began with two pre-arranged pieces prepared by members of Brendan's family.

Time and space were then left open for other informal contributions. Almost every person present spoke, some very briefly, others at length, of what they remembered and valued most of their unique relationship with Brendan.

We ended this part with two pieces, prepared by people whom Brendan had healed, one of whose spouse had died.

Closing and transition

Then the MC, David, read a piece about the season of the year, Samhain, and its symbolism of death and rebirth. I read the following piece from *The Hobbit* by Tolkien, which I felt was both helpful and appropriate:

> *Bilbo's Last Song*
> *(At the Grey Havens)*
> Day is ended, dim my eyes,
> but journey long before me lies.
> Farewell, friends! I hear the call.
>
> The ship's beside the stony wall
> beyond the sunset leads my way.
> Foam is salt, wind is free,
> I hear the rising of the sea.
>
> Farewell, Friends! The sails are set,
> the wind is east, the moorings fret,

shadows long before me lie
beneath the ever-bending sky,
but islands lie beyond the Sun
that I shall raise ere all is done,
lands there are to west of West
where night is quiet and sleep is rest.

Guided by the Lonely Star,
beyond the utmost harbour bar
I'll find the havens fair and free,
and beaches of the Starlet Sea.
Ship, my ship! I seek the West
and fields and mountains ever blest.
Farewell to middle-earth at last.
I see the Star above my mast!

David then explained that we would next move on to the scattering of Brendan's ashes.

Scattering of Brendan's ashes

Several carloads of those present travelled to a harbour, where a boat had been hired. David, members of Brendan's family and one or two others, boarded the boat with Brendan's ashes, while others remained watching from the shore.

When some way out to sea, a sensitive and sympathetic boatman turned off the engines, and David read the following:

> I am standing upon the seashore. A ship at my side spreads her white sails to the morning breeze and starts for the blue ocean. She is an object of beauty and strength; and I stand and watch her until at last she is only a ribbon of white cloud, just where the sea and sky come to mingle with each other. Then someone at my side says:
> 'There! She's gone!'
> 'Gone where?'
> Gone from my sight – that is all. She is just as large in mast and

hull and span as she was when she left my side, and just as able to bear her load of living freight to the place of destination. Her diminished size in me, not in her, and just at the moment when someone says 'There! She's gone!' there are other voices ready to take up the glad shout: 'There! She comes!'
And *that* is dying.

Then each person scattered a handful of ashes, and the remainder David poured out through the hands of Brendan's son. Others scattered single flowers on the sea. They remained for a time in silence before returning to the shore.

A participant, Anne Louise, observed that:

In the best of all worlds, each person in death should be honoured by a celebration, especially fashioned to remember their life.

and another, Desmond:

I have always loved swimming, and felt the sea is a mother. Therefore, it was most comforting to see Brendan's ashes going 'back' to the sea.

These three rituals, all very different, were chosen not for you to imitate, but perhaps to inspire you to create your own if you so wish, as just another way of moving through your grief.

PART V

LEARNING TO LIVE AGAIN

CHAPTER 13

RE-ENTRY, RE-ENGAGEMENT, RE-ATTACHMENT

Again the forest is fragrant
The soaring larks lift up aloft
With them the sky that to our
Shoulders was heavy.
(Rilke)

As I have said, the amount and intensity of grief we experience after a death will depend largely on the depth of the relationship, the degree of attachment we had to the deceased, and how much our identity was dependent on the relationship.

At different times in our lives we are attached to different people, places and things, appropriate to our age and circumstances. It is healthy, appropriate, even necessary for survival at times, to form these attachments. It can be unhealthy if they are inappropriate, or if we invest so much in them that we give away or lose part of our selves (see Chapter 14). When we have to move on, for any reason, from these attachments, or let them go, we experience separation and, consequently, pain. When we have completed the grieving, we are then free to attach again to another person, place or thing, and invest the energy elsewhere.

At the stage at which you have faced your loss, felt and expressed the pain, and are getting used to living without your beloved, you may believe you have done enough. Are you asking yourself 'Is it really necessary to keep trying? After all, it is such an effort'?

You may be thinking that you have done well to come so far; that life is so difficult, unfair, lonely and such a struggle anyway, that there is no point in working at it any more. Nothing will bring your loved one back, nothing will change that. You are coping, living a fairly normal life again, so why can you not just stay the way you are – coping, existing.

All of these feelings are normal at a certain stage. You have worked hard to get to this point, and you are probably very tired physically, as well as emotionally. Yes, nothing you can do will bring your loved one back; and life is difficult, unfair, sad and lonely at times. But, existing in this way is not the best you can expect. You have every right, and reason, to hope for more.

Can I Ever Love Again?

Is this a shocking question? Do you feel angry when you read it, or guilty, sad or hopeless, even impotent, despairing, or just plain scared? These feelings arise for many people. It is quite normal, but not an excuse to close your mind to new relationships.

If you are feeling guilty, or that it is disloyal to the deceased, remember love is limitless in its source. It never dries up, it only gets blocked by our own limitations. If you gave a lot of love to the one who has gone, there is just as much love there to give again. It is not the same piece of love. You are not taking away the love you had for the deceased and reinvesting it in someone new. Your love for the deceased was, and is, a part of you, which will never change.

If you are scared, perhaps of failing to make a new relationship, or making a mess of it, or just of the sheer effort required to begin building a relationship again from the beginning, do not let that stop you. Maybe you will 'fail' at first, or make mistakes, but you will be out there participating in life rather than observing or absenting yourself from it.

I mentioned previously the danger of making decisions to love again too soon after your loss. You must grieve first, you must do the grief work. Otherwise, you are 'applying another person to the wound' in order to cover up the pain. Often you are using them to forget your loved one when you cannot face the grieving. This is a mistake for both you and your 'new' love, and for the future of the relationship.

When I use the word 'love' in this context, I use it in its broadest sense, not in a romantic way. I intend to include relationships with babies, children, lovers, partners, spouses, friends and companions of all kinds.

Love is an energy, and it is that *energy* you will be reinvesting. If, for example, you have experienced the death of an elderly parent, obviously you cannot reinvest your energy in an exactly similar relationship. But you will probably have more of that type of energy to give to other relationships, for example, to your partner or children. You may invest in another elderly person who may meet some of the same needs your parent met for you.

Needs play a big part in love. We all have needs. That is part of being human, and we look to others to meet some of these needs. No one person can meet all our needs; that is an unreal and unfair expectation, and poisonous to any relationship.

When someone has died, you will never again find anyone to meet the exact combination of needs that she met. But you may find someone who will meet some of them, plus some others in a new combination. No two people will have all the same gifts, or faults.

Of course, there are many occasions when you cannot find anyone to meet the majority of those same needs. This is particularly true if you are older, when it may not be possible, or you may not wish, to make a new relationship. That is your choice and your right. The memories and what you still hold inside yourself of the deceased, are enough.

Comparison

If you do make the mistake of trying to replace the lost loved one with someone else, it will not work. You must obviously love a person for themselves. If they are a replacement, you will be constantly comparing them to the one you have lost. That is why you must grieve and let go of the original attachment. It is natural to make comparisons. It is not natural to expect one person to be the same as another, or to meet the same needs in you. Unreal expectations ruin a relationship, and it is unreal to expect any two people to be the same, or to fulfil exactly similar needs in us.

If it is one of your children that has died, no other child you already have, nor a new baby, will ever be the same as the one you have lost. Of course, you know that at a conscious level and so you will not consciously expect it. However, at an unconscious level, it may be different. Check it out with yourself. It can be disastrous for a child to grow up feeling that she is 'not enough', by not succeeding in filling the gap left by one who has died.

Venturing again: first steps

If it is a lover, spouse or partner who has died, although you cannot expect to meet someone similar or someone who will fill the same needs, you may be looking for someone to fill the same role in your life. In this case, it is easier to fall into the trap of comparisons. It can also happen that once the grieving is done, you become over-anxious to fill that gap in your life. Try to take your time. Know that you may have many relationships before you find someone who will fill that role.

Try to learn to enjoy life for itself rather than because you are sharing the experience with someone else. This is difficult at first, and, if you depend a lot for your enjoyment on sharing it, it may feel awkward, even empty. Persevere. It will feel different but not necessarily less enjoyable (see below and Chapter 15).

One of the strange paradoxes about this stage of grieving is that it is often only when you have achieved the strength to stand alone that you will find new relationships. If and when you do meet someone you like, take it slowly; for example, meet at intervals at first rather than becoming too serious too soon and rushing into a new commitment before you really know the person. Remember, no two people are ever the same, so no two relationships are ever the same. Do not expect them to be.

If you are hoping to make a relationship that will fill the role of the deceased, such as a spouse, keep reminding yourself that no two marriages or partnerships are ever the same. To give a new person in your life a chance, remember that you are creating a new life together. It is a partnership. It is not a case of you remaining the same and the new person 'fitting' in. This not only applies to personality and emotions, but to the house you lived in in your last partnership, the furnishings and decor and the friends you shared. You may keep some of them; you may not. But it is the two of you who must create all this again together. You must not slot him or her into the space left by the deceased.

If you feel you are ready for a new relationship, do not sit around and wait for Mr or Ms Right to appear. Involve yourself in activities that interest you, mix with old friends. Accept every invitation, within reason. These are the ways to meet new people. If you do not meet a new partner, you will be out there involved in what interests you in life, and living.

Couples

A lot of socialising is done on a couple basis, especially among the over-thirties. If you have been part of a couple, and through your bereavement now find yourself to be single again, this can put an additional strain on your step to re-enter any kind of social life. If this way of thinking, and socialising, operates in your circle, do not let it put you off. It is more difficult, but just another stumbling block to overcome.

It is my belief that if people cannot accept you for yourself, they are not worthy of your friendship. Get some courage by talking it over with a real friend, and then go out there and brave it. Remember, it will be nothing compared to what you have been through.

Final task of grieving

At this point, when you have begun to re-engage in life and reinvest in new relationships, you are completing the last task of grief work. You may be surprised that you are still experiencing, at times, some of the same feelings as in the early stages of grieving. That is quite normal. Even years and years after a death you will have flashes of all those early feelings: anger, guilt, depression, despair, even denial. If there are flashes, moments, or short and occasional periods of experiencing these feelings, that is normal. If they last for long periods or are interfering with your normal life, you would probably be helped by consulting a counsellor or psychotherapist.

CHAPTER 14

ETERNITY'S SUNRISE

He who binds to himself a joy
Does the winged life destroy;
He who kisses the Joy as it flies
Lives in Eternity's sunrise
(William Blake)

When your loved one died, in the early stages of grieving you may never have imagined that you would ever be happy or at peace again, that you could ever again experience joy.

However great your loss and the grief associated with it, if you have been able to regard the whole experience as a turning point, then you will find peace and joy, perhaps even greater than ever before, possibly very different, but you will find it.

> … a place that all of us must pass through at one time or another – what mystics call the piercing of the veil of illusion. It's the point where we truly recognise that our physical world is not the ultimate reality and we begin to turn inward to discover the true nature of existence. At these times we usually feel emotionally that we are hitting bottom, but as we actually hit the bottom we fall through a trap door into a bright new world – the realm of spiritual truth. Only by moving fully into the darkness can we move through it into the light.
> Shakti Gawain with Laurel King, *Living in the Light* (Eden Grove Editions)

Now, having come through the darkness of grief, having experienced this turning point, the time has come to leave behind the sorrow (not the memories), to let go and move on, to look forward to some light and joy in the future.

You may be feeling some twinges of guilt reading this. How can you even contemplate complete 'recovery' from your grief, not to mention joy!

Those twinges are the last dying embers of the grieving process, quite natural. Let them go. It is a big step; take courage. You cannot lose those who have died. It is no disrespect or disloyalty to the deceased to let them go, to undo those last emotional ties. If you feel you do not wish to take this step, do not lose heart. Take your time; each individual is different. You may never wish to make this break, or you may need to wait and grieve some more.

Let us now look at joy, how you can experience it as fully as possible, how you can 'let it in'. This involves various processes. The following are those that I consider to be the most central and most helpful in reclaiming joy after grief.

- Live in, and experience the moment.
- Know what you want and pursue it.
- Experience the joy for yourself, rather than for others.

Living In and Experiencing the Moment
Living on this planet is an experience not to be missed! Yet most of us fail to experience it as fully as our human potential allows. We miss experiencing what is actually happening to us just now because our attention is, to some extent, 'preoccupied', either with the past or the future, and, therefore, not focused fully on the experience of the moment.

'Preoccupation' with the past and future
When we are upset about a recent traumatic experience, we tend to think about it a lot, for example, when we have had a car accident, or someone close to us is seriously ill or has just died. Although the memory fades with time, the 'scar' left by the hurtful incident does not, unless it has been dealt with and integrated. Some of our attention or energy, therefore, is still focused on it, even though we are less and less aware of it as time passes. When, normally in a counselling or therapy session, we deal with the incident and, therefore, the 'scar', we release that energy or attention, which is then available for our present-day living. 'Preoccupation' with the past or the future can be unconscious or unaware. If your answer is 'yes' to any

of the following, you may be 'preoccupied' with the past or the future to some degree:

- Are you a 'worrier'?
- Are you anxious, but not sure what it's about?
- Are you conscious at times of a vague feeling of 'impending doom'?
- Do you hoard useless objects, memorabilia, old collections of cards, photographs, stamps, etc.?
- Is your wardrobe full of clothes you have not worn for over a year?
- Do you spend too much time reminiscing about the 'good old days'?
- Does your nostalgia interfere with your appreciating the world as it is now?
- Are there people whom you were separated from, or who died, many years ago, that you cannot let go?
- Do you worry obsessively or unduly about your health, old age or death?

Of course, we are shaped by our past and our memories, and reminders are very important for our psychological stability and health. It is about balance.

Do you suspect that there are some painful losses or events that you have not fully let go, that are holding you in the past – what is often called 'unfinished business'. If so, find a friend, counsellor or psychotherapist, and scan your life in terms of this unfinished business. Always start with the past, as far back as you can remember, and work up to the present. Note which events still evoke painful feelings, even if it is only the fact that they have passed and are gone that is painful.

Then, take each painful event and talk it out with your friend or therapist, accepting that it happened, facing it, grieving and letting it go. You may actually say the word 'goodbye'.

If you do not have a friend, counsellor or psychotherapist, you could do this on your own by writing or journalling. But it can be lonely and, therefore, increase the feelings of isolation. This process may take time. Do not hurry. It will be different for each one. If you take the time and courage to work through this process, it will allow you to let go emotionally.

Now to the physical letting go. Again, and this may surprise you, I'd suggest asking a friend to be with you. Clear out your attic, cupboards and drawers, your garages and garden sheds. Sort out your old postcards, photographs and other collections. Give away any clothes you haven't worn for eighteen months. Do all this slowly, and use the opportunity to let go of treasured items and say 'Goodbye' to them. It has to be a deliberate process, made with the will – not a mindless or haphazard clearout. We must deal with our past fears if we are to live fully, and that is no quick or easy task.

The future

It is important to deal with the past first, as this will help in dealing with the future. Worry and anxiety about the future are frequently caused by undealt with, or unresolved past trauma. However, much preoccupation with the future has its roots in an underlying fear of our own death or mortality. I believe it is quite normal to fear death, especially our own. Firstly, fear of our own death is part of our survival instinct, and, therefore, natural to all human animals. It is also fear of the unknown. Fear of the ending of our 'self' as most of us consciously experience it. That includes fear of letting go and leaving all that is familiar in the universe, including our homes, possessions and those we love. We fear the pain and suffering that has been an intrinsic part of dying since human life began, and for some people still is.

Although it is normal and usual to fear death, unless you have dealt with and integrated it, it will preoccupy or use up a lot of your energy and attention for living. You cannot remove these fears, but you can learn to live with them. They can be dealt with by acknowledging them, talking about them, allowing yourself to express any feelings associated with them, and then trying to live life without them. You may be able to do this with a friend, counsellor or psychotherapist.

Some practical steps you can take to help deal with them are as follows:

- Take good care of yourself physically, with diet, exercise, etc.
- See a doctor if you are worried about a health matter.
- Deal with any 'unfinished business' as described above.
- Make your will.
- Discuss your wishes for your affairs, funeral, etc. with family, friends or whoever will look after these for you.
- Visit people and places you have always wanted to visit, but haven't taken the time or trouble lately or even ever.
- Let your hair go grey, start to accept and be proud of your age.
- Start a new hobby, job or career, or even retire if you feel you are not living in tune with your 'soul'.

Once you have done this work, I believe much of your emotional and physical fear of death and the unknown will fall into proportion, though it will not disappear completely. The exercise of letting go of the past, which I have recommended above, will also contribute to alleviating these fears and also the fear of pain, suffering and the end of the self as we know it.

Death is the greatest letting-go of all. Letting go as we go along, and so engaging fully in 'living the now' is what helps, and prepares us for death.

Unconsciously, we let go many times every day in small ways. We must keep our attention somewhat in the present, in order to get up in the morning, eat, deal with the world, work, play, etc. As we move on in the day, we leave the immediate past behind, and let it go. We do this quite naturally, unless there is an emotional scar involved, which blocks this natural flow of life.

When these blocks occur, you need more time and energy before you can move on, and sometimes you may need help to do so, as I have described.

Life and circumstances often force us to face our hurts, and to move on. But we frequently avoid the step of feeling the hurts, and particularly the expression of the feelings, by talking about them and even crying or expressing anger.

Knowing What You Want and Pursuing it

Do you find it difficult to enjoy yourself, to take time just for you? If you do enjoy yourself, do you feel guilty? Do you have difficulty in knowing what you would like to do, given a choice? These difficulties probably have their roots in early childhood.

The values we grow up with are instrumental in shaping not only our views of the world, the human condition and the meaning of life itself, but how we see right from wrong.

We live in a society in which numerous institutions tell us what is good for us, what we should want. There are 'experts' who tell us what is good for our physical, mental, emotional and spiritual health. We are told how to achieve this health through medicine, education, religion and general lifestyle. We learn to believe, at a very deep level, that others – the experts – always know best. Most of us did not learn early on to 'tune into' ourselves, to trust this self to know, or find out, what we needed in order to 'march to the sound of our own drum', to 'play our own tune'. We were not trained to listen for the 'still small voice'.

Growing up in my family, I learned that what mattered most was 'doing good', serving others and leaving the world a better place when you die. The most important value was to love your neighbour, but never to love, or think about, yourself.

In school, I was told that I should deprive myself of what I wanted most, in order to make up for my own and others' sins.

These values are what influenced my adult views and behaviour. Each of us have had different influences, some good and some bad. Even if they appeared to be all good, they can have a bad effect. For example, the 'doing good and leaving the world a better place' was, in a sense, a good influence. But if being 'good' is what a child perceives she has to do to 'earn' love, as I did, then it can, but does not necessarily, become a compulsion. As an adult, that child may have difficulty in making a free choice to do what she perceives to be 'good'. As a result, either this perception of good may be distorted, or she may behave compulsively or irrationally, for example, by over-working to the point of damaging her health.

If you have any of these difficulties, that is, in enjoying yourself, feeling guilty if you do, knowing what you want and what is best for you and pursuing it, then what can you do? I suggest some or all of the following:

- Acknowledge the particular difficulty.
- Trace its origins and talk it out.
- Practise the 'new you'.

If you can acknowledge any of these difficulties, that is the most important step. Once you can recognise the difficulty and are aware of it, you are halfway there. For some, that alone is enough. Remember, what you are aiming at is freedom to make the decisions you really want to make, not necessarily a new and 'remodelled' you. Sometimes, however, acknowledgement and awareness are not enough.

Tracing the origins of the difficulty or difficulties can be done in discussion with a friend, counsellor or psychotherapist. Once you have the awareness that the 'block' is there, it is usually quite simple to identify when and how it originated. This can also be done on your own by reflection. Try meditation or simply taking time on your own to get in touch with your 'self' and to listen to the 'still small voice'. Keeping a daily diary of your thoughts and feelings can also be useful.

More talking or writing may be necessary to tease out the details of how this is affecting you. Once you have found the early blocks, you often realise in how many subtle ways these blocks are affecting your behaviour apart from the way you originally identified. If this feels very difficult, or is very upsetting, that is quite normal, but you may find it useful to consult a counsellor or psychotherapist.

Finally, you must practise how to live without these blocks. It will not be easy. At this point, joining an assertiveness class can be useful. Contrary to common perception, assertiveness is not about 'getting your own way' or being selfish or insensitive to others' wishes. Assertiveness is about what I have been discussing above, that is, understanding yourself and finding out what is best for you.

Practising living without the blocks can mean learning to live with guilt for a time. If experiencing joy in your life, or doing what you believe to be right for you, has made you feel guilty all your life, the guilt will not disappear overnight. It should fade slowly with practice, and perhaps doing some more quiet reflection or meditation on an ongoing basis. You may wish to continue sharing with a counsellor or psychotherapist, or journalling about the guilt.

Practising to live in a new way affects those around you. Often they are delighted, but sometimes they do not like the 'new you', or do not know how to relate to you in a new way. This can be the cause of quite a disruption in your life. Do not be put off. You may wish to explain to those close to you what is happening. They may or may not understand. They will adjust slowly and learn how to relate differently, as you are doing. But it takes time. Be prepared for the upheaval.

To summarise, check if you have difficulty with any of the following:

- Enjoying yourself.
- Enjoying yourself without feeling guilty.
- Taking time for yourself.
- Knowing what is best for you.
- Doing what is best for you.

If so, you may like to try:

- Acknowledging the difficulty.
- Tracing its origin and talking it out, with a friend, counsellor or psychotherapist.
- Taking time alone to reflect, meditate or journal.
- Developing a sense of 'self'.
- Taking an assertiveness class.
- Learning to live with guilt.
- Expecting and dealing with upheaval in your relationships.

Experiencing the Joy for Yourself

I have written elsewhere about learning to do things slowly without your loved one, either alone or with different people. Having travelled that path, you know that it is not easy. The next step is to learn to enjoy yourself with people other than the deceased, or on your own.

How easy, or difficult, this step is, depends largely on the type of relationship you had with the deceased. If you were dependent on her for your enjoyment, or even more, if you relied on her for the very meaning of your existence, then you will need to work hard in order to live fully and enjoy living fully for yourself.

If your relationship was an over-dependent one, it is even easier to fall into the trap I mentioned in Chapter 13 of 'applying another person to the wound', rather than helping and allowing the wound to heal first. This type of dependency in a relationship often comes from a lack of self-worth, or an undeveloped sense of self in the dependent partner.

This sense of self can be developed in many ways, through prayer, meditation, psychotherapy, counselling, friendship, marriage or committed relationship, or simply by dealing with the ups and downs of life itself. It is a long journey to the self – think of all the metaphors and allegorical folk takes in so many cultures.

Finding out what you want, pursuing it and becoming an independent self can cause a lot of disruption in your life, particularly in relationships. Again, explaining some of what is happening to you may help, but do not let this disruption daunt you. The pursuit of self is a difficult and long journey, but there is no other more rewarding.

When you want to try enjoying things without the deceased, start in small ways, and do not expect too much of yourself. Each step will remind you of many past times your beloved was with you, and you may need to grieve some more as you go along.

Begin by sharing the outing or event with someone close, and tell them how you are feeling. Then, try taking different people, and not telling them how you are feeling. Finally, venture on your own. It may seem strange at first, but persevere. Start with things you like to do most, that you almost can't help enjoying, even on your own. All of this takes time: be patient.

To conclude, remember, all of this focus on joy is about getting a balance in your life. It is about being able to make choices about what you do, as free as possible from early conditioning. It is not about pursuing joy to the exclusion of all else and all others. It is about living in Eternity's sunrise.

BIBLIOGRAPHY

Eliot, T. S., *The Four Quartets* (London: Faber and Faber, 1959).

Feinstein, David and Elliot Mayo, Peg, *Rituals for Living and Dying* (San Francisco: Harper, 1990).

Frankl, Victor E., *Man's Search for Meaning* (London: Hodder, 1987).

Gawain, Shakti with King, Laurel, *Living in the Light* (London: Eden Grove Editions, 1988).

Gibran, Kahlil, *The Prophet* (London: Pan Books, 1991).

Hinton, John, *Dying* (London: Pelican, 1967).

Jackins, Harvey, *The Human Side of Human Beings* (Seattle: Rational Island Publishers, 1978).

Krenientz, Jill, *How It Feels When A Parent Dies* (London: Victor Gollancz, 1983).

Kübler-Ross, Elisabeth, *On Death and Dying* (London: Tavistock Publications, 1970).

Kushner, Harold S., *When Bad Things Happen to Good People* (London: Pan Books, 1982).

Lampen, Diana, *Facing Death* (Quaker Home Service).

Lewis, C. S., *A Grief Observed* (London: Faber and Faber, 1961).

Murray Parkes, Colin, *Bereavement* (London: Pelican, 1962).

Pincus, Lily, *Death and the Family* (London: Faber and Faber).

Worden, William J., *Grief Counselling and Grief Therapy* (London: Tavistock Publications, 1993).

Young Brown, Molly, *The Unfolding Self: Psychosynthesis and Counselling* (Los Angeles: Psychosynthesis Press, 1983).

Zappone, Katherine, *The Hope for Wholeness* (Mystic CT: Twenty-Third Publications, 1991).

INDEX